"WESTWARD THE COURSE OF EMPIRE"

EXPLORING AND SETTLING THE AMERICAN WEST

1803–1869

“WESTWARD THE COURSE OF EMPIRE”

EXPLORING AND SETTLING THE AMERICAN WEST

1803–1869

Books & Maps from the Collection of

J. C. McELVEEN, Jr.

THE GROLIER CLUB

NEW YORK

2018

Catalogue of an exhibition held at the Grolier Club

March 21–May 26, 2018

COVER: One of many images reproduced or adapted from John Gast's painting *American Progress* (1872), depicting an allegorical female figure of America towering over settlers and pioneers, and wagons and railroads, as she leads the way westward. From *Chase & Bachelder's American Museum of Art,* [c. 1875] (fig. 68).

ISBN 978-1-60583-073-5

CONTENTS

FOREWORD

THE AMERICAN WEST remained a mysterious region during the early exploration and settlement of North America. Its vast distances, endless rolling grasslands, majestic mountains, imposing tablelands, and countless roiling rivers stirred the imagination of the first explorers and settlers, but slowed their advance.

The exhibition *"Westward the Course of Empire": Exploring and Settling the American West 1803–1869* illustrates this story with contemporary maps and journals from the personal collection of J. C. McElveen, who also curated the event. Following his retirement from a noted Washington, DC law firm, Mr. McElveen augmented his knowledge of western cartography as a volunteer in the Geography and Map Division of the Library of Congress describing its vast collection of early maps of the American West.

Maps are compelling documents for conceptualizing time and space. "Nothing can evoke a moment like a map," Welsh historian and travel writer Jan Morris has written.[1] Geographer Anne Godlewska observed that the map is "a synthesis of information which is a great deal more than just a collection of facts about places."[2]

Prof. Godlewska lists several sources contributing to the power of maps that are relevant to our understanding of early Western exploration and settlement cartography. First, maps illustrate not only what is known or perceived about a place or region but also that which is unknown. Further, since maps convey information pictorially through words, symbols and colors, they are interpreted situationally "as we perceive the world around us" rather than read linearly as a book. This leads to more direct and easier communication with maps than with textual documents. Another characteristic of their power is that map information is greatly generalized in hierarchical form. Coastlines, rivers, paths and roads are straightened; pictorial sketches or contours depict the essential features of mountains and hills. Fourth, maps hold complex and multiple layers of information through words, symbols and colors that illustrate intricate geographical, historical and cultural themes. Next, the precision of the lines and grids on maps suggest a level of scientific accuracy and objectivity that may not always be supported by the subjective nature of nineteenth century cartography. Finally, maps often reflect the biases and belief systems of their producers or patrons, or the particular set of the political, social and economic systems of their era.[3]

---

1. Jan Morris, "On Maps," 5.4 *Asian Art* (Fall, 1992): 3.
2. Anne Godlewska, "Commentary: The Fascination of Jesuit Cartography." In *Jesuit Encounters in the New World: Jesuit Chroniclers, Geographers, Educators and Missionaries in the Americas, 1549–1767,* edited by Joseph A. Gagliano and Charles E. Ronan. Rome: Institutum Historicum S.I., 1997: 99–104.
3. J. Brian Harley, "Deconstruction of the Map," *Cartographia* 26, 2 (1989): 1–20.

To my knowledge this is the first map exhibition by a private collector devoted to the opening of the American West. It is also appropriate that it opens in the bicentenary anniversary of the formal establishment of the US Army's Topographical Bureau and Map Unit (later the Corps of Topographical Engineers), which contributed significantly to the mapping of the West.

Although this exhibition reflects the interests of one collector, Mr. McElveen's selection of maps and journals is very comprehensive, ranging from the decorative and intellectually provocative European maps of the seventeenth and eighteen centuries to the science-based topographic maps of the nineteenth century, with their mathematically constructed grids of geographic latitude and longitude that display only essential wayfinding elements such as distances, directions, place names, and political divisions. It is enhanced with judiciously selected journal entries and engaging illustrations.

The contrast between decorative and scientific maps is only one of the exhibit's many interesting features. Comparing maps produced by field explorers such as Alexander Mackenzie and William Clark with those compiled by the commercial publishers who incorporate the explorer's data raise interesting questions of accuracy and inclusiveness. Mr. McElveen raises several other questions that his exhibition may spark in his Preface.

Viewers of this exhibition will leave with a much greater awareness of the early exploration of the American West, and a better insight of the role that maps and mapmakers played in this process.

Ralph E. Ehrenberg
Chief, Geography and Map Division, Retired
Library of Congress

PREFACE

I HAVE ALWAYS always loved American history and, for me, maps were often helpful in visualizing battles, explorations and demographic and societal changes, such as the movement to cities. I was also fascinated by the idea that maps could convey an enormous amount of information in a small space. As well, a number of them were very attractive. So, I began to acquire a few maps, then a few more, and then . . . well you know the rest of *that* story.

Given my interest, it is not too surprising that when I began collecting maps, my attention was focused on those that illustrated various aspects of the history of North America. However, the breadth of that collecting area was extremely daunting. What to collect? Wars? Which ones? The American Revolution, the Civil War, World War II? A particular city, state or region? Maps on specific topics, such as geology, agriculture, national improvements? As it turned out, the question answered itself.

The first map I ever bought was a fairly well known 1719 French map of the Western Hemisphere. I bought it because it spoke to me. I bought it because it had beautiful graphics, illustrating everything from mining to cod fishing to beaver hunting. I bought it because it combined art and information in a beautiful and relatively compact form. In short, it was a one-map history of the European vision of North and South America in the first half of the eighteenth century.

But the map had some intriguing oddities, as well. For example, California was shown as an island. Except for the "Riviere du Norte ou Brave" (later called the Rio Grande), there were no major rivers west of the Mississippi on this map. There were no Rocky Mountains, or Cascades—and almost all of what we now call "the West" was blank. On a 1720 English-language map I acquired shortly thereafter, that latter problem was solved by the mapmaker labeling the bulk of the West as "Parts Unknown." Following this lengthening trail of questions, I then bought a map that, above where Texas would later be found, bore the notation: "Wandering Indians and Man-Eaters." These maps now had my full attention.

When and how did California "become" an island, and how did it get re-attached to the North American continent? When and how did the Missouri and the Platte and the Gila and the Colorado and the Columbia Rivers get put on the map? When and how did "Parts Unknown" get filled in? When did people decide that getting to the Pacific Ocean wasn't going to be as easy as crossing the Alleghenies? Those questions raised others. What was it about the West? When someone says to you, "Let's go someplace and, on the way, you might drown in a river, starve, or die of thirst in a desert, freeze to death on a mountain (yes, Mr. Donner, I'm talking to you), or be killed by unfriendly natives," why would you say, "Yeah, that sounds like a great idea!" What caused people to say to their families, "I'll probably never see you again," buy a bunch of mules or oxen they had no idea how to control, get aboard a wagon they had no idea how to fix if it broke down, and set off on a two- or three-thousand-mile journey across some of the most inhospitable terrain in the world?

My maps and the questions they generated led me to seek out (and, of course, collect) the reports and accounts of these journeys, and to read about the hazards, the triumphs, and the thrills of the westward movement.

"*Westward the Course of Empire*," the title of this catalogue and related exhibition, is borrowed from the first part of the title of a mural displayed in the US Capitol, *Westward the Course of Empire Takes its Way*, by German immigrant painter Emanuel Leutze (1816–68). Completed in 1862, the mural depicts wagon trains of emigrants to the West at an idealized Continental Divide, looking toward a sun-dappled Pacific coast. This mural is one of many visual representations of Manifest Destiny, the theme that runs through this catalogue. The name of the mural is itself a line from a poem by Irish philosopher George Berkeley (1685–1753), "Verses on the Prospect of Planting Arts and Learning in America" (1726).[4]

I hope this catalogue will allow you to come along on this journey west, as you look at the images from early Spanish explorations to Lewis and Clark, to the US Army, to the scientists who helped chart the path for a transcontinental railroad. It has been a great ride for me.

J. C. McElveen

---

4. Architect of the Capitol. *Compilation of Works of Art and Other Objects in the United States Capitol, 86th Cong., 2nd Sess., House Document No. 162* (Washington, DC: Government Printing Office, 1965). For a more complete discussion of this art, see americanart.si.edu/t2go/1lw/1931.6.1.html (accessed August 13, 2017).

ACKNOWLEDGMENTS

MANY PEOPLE have been extremely helpful to me in bringing this catalogue and exhibition to fruition, and I want to express my everlasting gratitude to them. Ralph Ehrenberg, recently retired chief of the Geography and Map Division of the Library of Congress, and an expert on Lewis and Clark, first stimulated my interest in the mapping of western exploration and showed me many wonders. Anthony Mullan, Diane Schug-O'Neill and Mike Klein, also of the Geography and Map Division, pointed me to fabulous examples of western exploration and mapping. Dealers Barry Lawrence Ruderman, Eliane and Jon Dotson, and Harry Newman have offered me gorgeous examples of important objects, at affordable prices.

This catalogue would never have materialized if it had not been for Fern Cohen, the chair of the Grolier Club Member Exhibitions Committee, who encouraged me to submit a proposal. I also received encouragement and sage advice from Natalie and John Blaney, Tom Touchton and PJ Mode. And I also thank Grolier Club Director Eric Holzenberg and Exhibitions Manager Jennifer Sheehan for their continuing support throughout this endeavor.

I had a great deal of help with my images. Early on, my close friend Larry Rood, photographer par excellence, provided me with a number of very high quality images. Swann Auction Galleries, Barry Lawrence Ruderman Rare Maps, and the Old Print Gallery sent me outstanding high-resolution images. Old World Auctions personnel were kind enough to scan a number of images for me. Franz Jantzen (Archivalman) did some very detailed photos, which have greatly enhanced parts of the catalogue.

As I reviewed catalogues of earlier member exhibits, two names were mentioned in Acknowledgment sections again and again. Those names were George Ong as editor and Jerry Kelly as catalogue designer. Based on the fact that these catalogues were beautifully put together and the text and notes read like a dream, I contacted George and Jerry, and they kindly agreed to help me with this opus. They have been wonderful. What is right about this catalogue is because of them.

Finally, I owe a great debt to my wife, Mary. She put up with my research; she put up with my writing; she read my drafts; she made helpful suggestions. We are still married.

J. C. McElveen
August 6, 2017

I

IMAGINING NORTH AMERICA BEFORE THE NEW NATION

THE 16TH- AND 17TH-CENTURY SOUTHWEST

BEGINNING in the early sixteenth century and continuing into the eighteenth, the Spanish explored and settled what is now the southwestern United States, including parts of California, New Mexico, present-day Arizona and Texas. Having discovered great riches early in their explorations in Mexico and South America, they were reluctant to disclose or share the maps they drew of the American Southwest, in the event that valuable resources would be discovered there as well. Therefore, few Spanish maps were made public during that timeframe. However, because mapmakers disliked large blank areas on maps, many of them, as early as the mid-sixteenth century, inserted their own text on maps they made of the area. Some of these texts and names were based on data gathered from explorers who were willing to share it, like Sir Francis Drake, who landed on the west coast of North America in 1579; some of them were based on books written or tales told by explorers (or those who claimed to be explorers); and some of them were simply fabricated in their entirety.

Many of the early maps bear unfamiliar names such as Anian, Cibola (or Civola), and the kingdoms of Quivira and Tolm. Anian was the name given to either the body of water separating North America and Asia, or the western end of what many believed was a northwest passage across North America. The name may have derived from Marco Polo's name for a Chinese province, Ania. Cibola was an early name for the mythical Seven Cities of Gold, for which early Spanish soldiers were searching in the Southwest. As Spaniards explored the Southwest, they began to hear Native American descriptions of cities with great riches. In the early 1540s, Francisco Vásquez de Coronado sought out such a city, called Quivira; however, he only found Native American villages and pueblos.

East of Baja California is a body of water often called "Mare Vermeto," or Vermeio (the Vermillion Sea), so named because algae in the water made the water look red. Geographic representational distortions are also found in very early maps of North and South America, particularly along their western coasts; mountains are shown going along an east-west axis, instead of north-south; several large rivers run east and west, and there is no Mississippi River.

However, there are also features on these maps that are quite accurate or familiar. California is named on maps as early as 1587. Prior to the 1620s, it is shown as a peninsula (as opposed to an island, discussed below). There is some form of a river from the north running into what would later be named the Gulf of California, as the Colorado River would ultimately be shown to do (often, that river is called the Axa River or the Tizon River and is frequently quite short). A river from the east flows into the Gulf of California, which tracks the Gila River pretty well, though that river is often called the River of the Martyrs. The words "Sierra Nevada" (snowy mountains) are used, though they are not always associated with mountains. And "Hispania Nova," or New Spain, is identified (figs. 1 and 2).

CALIFORNIA AS AN ISLAND

Beginning in the early 1620s, perhaps the oddest North American cartographical misrepresentation began to appear on many maps of the West—California as an island. Although very early maps of the Pacific coast of North America showed California, correctly, as being attached to the North American continent, an English mapmaker, Henry Briggs, showed it as an island on a 1625 map, and many mapmakers over the next hundred years followed suit. Briggs may have borrowed the idea from a Spanish map he had seen in the early 1620s, figuring that the Spanish, who had explored much of that part of the world, must know what they were doing. No one is certain why anyone thought California was an island. It is possible that some Spaniards sailed up the Gulf of California, never got as far as the Colorado River and assumed California was an island (figs. 3 and 4). During this period, of course, almost no one knew the exact topography of most of the major land and water features of western North America, and some mapmakers just put features on maps where they thought they ought to be. For example, in a number of maps, though the Mississippi River is shown as emptying out into the Gulf of Mexico, it is shown as doing so from Texas, far west of where its mouth is actually located. Finally, in the late 1600s, Father Eusebio Kino, a Jesuit missionary, traveled from Santa Fe to California, proving that California was not an island. His map, originally published in the *Lettres edifiantes et curieuses, ecrites des missions etrangeres* [Jesuit Letters] (1705) and reprinted many times over the next decades, tried to convey that point visually (fig. 5). However, it was not until the king of Spain decreed in 1746 that California was not an island that the practice of showing it as one was eliminated.

THE 16TH- AND 17TH-CENTURY NORTHWEST

From the very beginnings of exploration of the North American continent there had been a hope, and even an expectation, that there would be a water route across the continent. Initially, it was postulated that the passage would cut across the northern part of the continent, and in many early maps and treatises, it was referred to as the "northwest passage." In one tale, periodically trotted out between 1708 and 1752, a Spanish admiral, Bartholomew de Fonte, was said to have sailed up the west coast of North America in 1650, into a river at 53 degrees north latitude (in present-day British Columbia). As he was sailing east, he encountered a ship heading west from Boston.

As time passed and no passage across the northern part of the continent could be found, it was speculated that perhaps a river flowed across the West and into the Pacific that could easily be accessed, after a short portage, from the source of one of the major eastern rivers. This purported western-flowing river was labeled "River of the West" or the "Buenaventura River," among other names. Though no easy water passage across North America was ever discovered, the legend persisted.

A very popular book and accompanying map by Louis-Armand de Lom d'Arce, Baron de Lahontan (1666–1716) helped keep that myth alive. Baron de Lahontan served in the French army in Canada in the late seventeenth century and was involved in some explorations in present-day Wisconsin. His book, *New Voyages to North-America* (London, 1703), chronicled his adventures in North America. The first part of the work was in the form of rather lengthy letters he purportedly wrote to some colleagues, and one has always been of particular interest: Letter XVI (Missilimakinac, May 28, 1689). There he described a trip he took, in 1688, down the Mississippi River and then northwest up another large river, for several hundred miles. He called this river the Longue River, or the Morte River. He told of meeting up along this river with Native Americans from a tribe he called the Gnacsitares, who described another, very aggressive tribe, located further west, called the Mozeemlek. Four Mozeemlek captives provided him with "a description of their country," with their villages standing "upon a [westward-flowing] river that springs out of a ridge of mountains from which the long river also derives its source."[5] The captives proceeded to tell Lahontan that the river on which they lived emptied "it self into a Salt Lake of three hundred leagues in circumference." The letter went on to describe the mountains of which the Mozeemleks spoke as being "six leagues broad and so high that one must cast an Infinity of Windings and Turnings before he can cross 'em."[6] The map that accompanied these descriptions even showed the portage from the source of the eastward-flowing "Longue River" to the westward-flowing river (fig. 6).

There is no documentation for Baron de Lahontan's trip, only his word that it occurred, and many believe that his was just another tall tale. However, some scholars have opined that he may well have had contact with Native Americans who told him about the height and ruggedness of the Rocky Mountains and described the Great Salt Lake of Utah. In any event, his book and map served to perpetuate the belief that there was a river route across much of the North American continent.

---

5. Louis-Armand de Lom d'Arce, Baron Lahontan, *New Voyages to North America*, vol. 1, 2nd ed. (London: John Brindley, 1735), 124–5.
6. Ibid.

THE 18TH-CENTURY WEST

By 1720, considerably more was known about the West, but much was yet to be discovered. That year, Herman Moll, a London cartographer and engraver, published a large map of the entire North American continent (fig. 7). Since Moll's map was produced, in part, to support British claims in North America against the French, the far West was not of particular importance to him. However, he did extend the coverage of his map to the Pacific. And consistent with contemporary knowledge (or lack thereof), he labeled almost all of the upper portion of the far West as "Parts Unknown." In the Southwest, California was shown as an island, even though this map was done after Father Kino's journey to California and the publication of his map. A foreshortened Colorado River—here referred to as the Tijon—was shown. A small river, further east, was labeled the "Coborado." The Rio Grande (with a part of its length the "Rio Del Norte" and another part, the "Rio Bravo") was also identified. Mountains appeared scattered throughout New Mexico, and various Native American tribes were identified across the continent: the Panis (Pawnee), Sioux, Apache, Padoucas (Comanche), Pima, Navajo, and many others. In the Northwest, the last segment of Baron de Lahonton's journey is shown, and the headwaters of the Mississippi appear several hundred miles too far west.

In 1718, Guillaume Delisle (sometimes "De L'Isle") of Paris published what was to be a seminal map that covered most of North America, *Carte de la Louisiane et du cours du Mississipi* . . . Its importance is due to its fairly accurate portrayal of the course of the Mississippi River and its tributaries, the Spanish territories to the Rio Grande and the Missouri River to the Great Bend at the Mandan Indian Villages. It was also the first printed map to identify Texas. Over the next several decades Delisle's map was widely copied, frequently word for word and line for line, and often without attribution. English publisher John Senex produced a verbatim English-language version of Delisle's map three years after its original publication (without attribution) (fig. 8).

Jonathan Carver, a British subject who fought in the French and Indian War, spent three years (1766–68) exploring the upper Midwest, going as far as the headwaters of the St. Peter's River. After he completed his travels, he wrote and published an account of them in *Travels Through the Interior Parts of North-America, in the Years 1766, 1767, and 1768* (London, 1778). The book was enormously popular, and it was frequently reprinted. Carver's book is important for a number of reasons. It contained the first appearance of "Oregon" in print. *Travels* also included maps that showed a River of the West that linked the Midwest to the Pacific Ocean (fig. 9), although this was simply a continuation of the wishful thinking that there was an easy way across the North American continent. A later Carver map, published in London in 1781, showed eleven numbered "states" in what would come to be called the Northwest Territory (fig. 10). (This was remarkably prescient, since Revolutionary War hostilities had barely ended by this point, and the Treaty of Paris between the United States and Britain was two years away. It wasn't until 1784 that Thomas Jefferson proposed a number of new states for the same territory.) Finally, Carver made one of the most far-reaching predictions about the American West when he said, apparently based solely on what Native Americans told him:

That range of mountains, of which the Shining (Rocky) Mountains are a part . . . is calculated to be more than three thousand miles in length, without any considerable intervals . . . Probably in future ages, they may be found to contain more riches in their bowels than those of Indostan and Malabar . . . to the west of these mountains, when explored by future Columbuses or Raleighs, may be found other lakes, rivers and countries, full fraught with all the necessities or luxuries of life; and where future generations may find an asylum, whether driven from their country by the ravages of lawless tyrants, or by religious persecutions, or reluctantly leaving it to remedy the inconveniences arising from a superabundant increase of inhabitants; whether, I say, impelled by these, or allured by hopes of commercial advantage, there is little doubt but their expectations will be fully gratified in these rich and unexhausted climes.[7]

7. Jonathan Carver, *Travels Through the Interior Parts of North America in the Years 1766, 1767 and 1768*, 3rd ed. (London: C. Dilly, 1781), 121–2.

AMERICA.
Anian.
Vlterius Septentrionem uersus hę regiones incognitę ad huc sunt.
SEPTENTRIO.
Terra Corte realis.
Saguenai
Canada
NOVA FRANCIA
Chilaga
Estotilant
Icaria
Frislant
Dos Demonios
Dus Cirnes
S. Brandani
Quiuira.
Sierra neuada.
Tuchano
Quiuirca
Tolm.
Cicuic
Toton
teac.
Marata.
Tiguas Rio
Suala Mons
Norumbega
Mocosa
Auacal
Calicuas
Tagil
Capaschi
Cossa
Apalchen
La Florida
C. de S. Iouan
Claudia
Arredonda
Baccalaos
Dobretan
y. de garca
S. Michel
Las Acores
Santana
Sept cites
La Bermuda
HISPANIA NOVA.
Topira
Mexico
Mecuacan
Tecoantepec
Zalisco
Guatalan
Cuba
Iucatan
Hispaniola
Iamaica
C. Californa
Rocca partida
MAR DEL ZVR
Circulus Aequinoctialis
Las dos hermanos
Los balcones
Malabrigos
La farfana
Restinga de ladrones
Zamal
Los Iardines
Ins. de las corales
Ins. de los Rays
MARE ATLANTICVM
y. de capo Verde
Dominica
Acripana
Ancon
Caribana
Quito
Cartago
Benezuela
Aldea
Tisnada
Atauali
Tumbes
Motupe
Trugilo
P. uermegio
Hacari
Cusco
PERV
Paguana
Amazones
Picora
Bresilia
C. Frio
Parana
Charcas
Chinca
Coquinbo
Ningatas
Patagonum regio
Chile
Chicha
Atacama
C. Blanco
Rio della Plata
C. de S. Augustin
Porto real
Ascention
S. maria
La barbuda
La Caimana
Los bolcanes
y. de los Tiburones
Hę duę insulę infortunatę sunt dictę a Magellano, quod nec homines nec uictui apta haberent
S. Petro
Hic Vspiam insulas esse, Auro diuites nonnulli uolunt
MARE PACIFICO
NOVA GVINEA
Andrea Corsalus Florent: Videtur eā sub nomine Terrę Piccinnacoli designare.
C. Hermoso
R. de S. Augustin
R. de S. Lorenzo
R. de Volcanes
Lucengo
Fretum Magellanicu
Terra del fuego.
C. di Maestro
Golfo de S. Sebastiano
R. de S. Croce
190 200 210 220 230 240 250 260 270 280 290 300 310 320 330 340 350 360

1

GIOVANNI ANTONIO MAGINI (1555–1617) · *AMERICA*

Venice: G. A. Magini, 1597. Copperplate engraving, 5 x 6⅞ in. From: G. A. Magini and Leonardo Cernoti, *Geografia cioe descrittione universale della Terra . . . Nuovamente* (Venice: Giovanni Battista Magini and Giorgio Galignani, 1597).

Giovanni Magini was a professor of astronomy, astrology and mathematics at the University of Bologna. This is a very early example of a map that uses the name "California." It also shows California as a peninsula, and identifies "Sierra Nevada," though no mountains are nearby. Many other geographical details are incorrect.

2

SEBASTIAN MUENSTER (1489–1552)
AMERICÆ SIVE NOVI ORBIS NOVA DESCRIPTIO / DIE NEWEN INSELN, SO HINDER HISPANIA GEGEN ORIENT, BEY DEM LANDT INDIE GELEGEN

Woodcut engraving, 14 x 12 in. From: *Cosmographia* (Basel: Sebastian Petri, 1614).

Sebastian Muenster was a German-born cartographer and Hebrew scholar who spent much of his adult life teaching in Basel, Switzerland. This map was originally published in Muenster's very popular description of the world, *Cosmographia* (1588), which continued to be published in revised editions until 1628.

Die newen Inseln/ so hinder Hispania gegen Orient/ bey dem Landt Indie gelegen.
SEPTENTRIO
Die newe Welt wird also genannt / von wegen der newen erfindung anno Domini 1492. beschehen / vnnd von wegen jhrer grösse / daß sie die eine halbe Kugel des Erdtrichs in die Weitlenge vnd breite beschleußt/ wie wol sie der breite nach dieser zeit noch nicht gar erkundigt ist.
Bresilien / so vber den equinoctial im Mittag gelegen / hat der König von Portugal inne: Noua Francia in Septentrion gelegen / ist vnder der Frantzosen Herrschafft: Das vbrige ist dem König in Spanien angehörig.
Vlterius Septentrionem Versus he Regiones Incognite ad huc sunt
ANIAN
TOLM
QVIVIRA
SAGENAI
NOVA
FRANCIA
Tiguas rio
TERLICHIMECHI
IOVA
HISPANIA NOVA
MARE VERMEIO
ARCHIPEAGO DI SAN LAZARO
CIRCVLVS ÆQVINOCTIALIS
MARE ATLANTICVM
OCCIDENS
ORIENS
PERV
CHARCAS
PARANA
PERSILIA
NOVA GVINEA
Andreas Coesalus Florent. Videtur eam sub nomine Terre Piccinnacoli designare
Hic Vsiam Insulas esse auro divites non nulli volunt
MARE PACIFICO
FRETVM MAGELLANICVM
MERIDIES
TERRA DEL FVEGO
AMERICÆ SIVE NOVI ORBIS, NOVA DESCRIPTIO
MERIDIES

3

PIERRE DUVAL (1618–1683) · *NOWEAV MEXIQVE*

Copperplate engraving, 4¾ x 4 in. From: *Le monde, ou La geographie universelle: Contenant les descriptions, les cartes, et le blason, de principaux païs du monde* (Paris: Pierre Duval, 1676).

This French map is a part of a world atlas. California is shown as an island; the Rio Nort (Rio Grande) is shown issuing from Lake Conibas, located in an area in what is now Colorado, and emptying into the Mer Vermeille (Gulf of California). However, Lake Conibas never existed, and the Rio Grande empties out into the Gulf of Mexico, not the Gulf of California. Some place names have stayed with us, however: Monterey, Cabo San Lucas, San Clemente Island and Point Sir Francis Drake. (Drake had sailed around the world from 1577–80, during which he explored the coast of California and named it New Albion); and the term "Apaches" (from the Zuni language, "enemies") is used to identify one of the Native American tribes.

4

HEINRICH SCHERER (1628–1704) · *AMERICA BOREALIS*

Munich, 1699. Copperplate engraving, 14 x 9 in. From: *Atlas novus* (Munich: Heinrich Scherer, 1703).

In this map, Scherer, a professor of mathematics at the University of Dillingen, showed the West as it was then understood. As was the case in the Duval map, California was shown as an island. In the East, as well, Scherer was behind the times: he referred to New York as New Amsterdam, even though the name was changed in 1664. However, Scherer's maps were among the first to show mountains through most of the West.

5

FATHER EUSEBIO FRANCISCO KINO (1645–1711) · *TABULA CALIFORNIAE ANNO 1702. EX AUTOPTICA OBSERVATIONE DELINEATA À R. P. CHINO, È S. I.*

Copperplate engraving, 18⅝ x 13½ in. From: Joseph Stöcklein, ed. *Der Neue Welt-Bott* (Augsburg: Veith, 1726).

Father Kino was an Italian Jesuit missionary who was assigned to Mexico. He spent much of his time working with Native Americans in an area called the Pimería Alta (northern Sonora, in Mexico, and modern-day Arizona). From 1698 until 1701, he led several expeditions from that area to California. This, his seminal map, was first drawn in 1702 and published in the *Lettres edifiantes et curieurses, ecrites des missions* [the Jesuit Letters] in 1705. However, it did not receive widespread publicity until it was published in Augsburg, Germany, in 1726.

6

HERMAN MOLL (1654?–1732) · *A MAP OF YE LONG RIVER AND OF SOME OTHERS THAT FALL INTO THAT SMALL PART OF YE GREAT RIVER OF MISSISIPI WICH IS HERE LAID DOWN*

Copperplate engraving, 14 x 10½ in. From: Louis-Armand de Lom d'Arce de Lahontan, Baron de Lahontan, *New Voyages to North-America, Giving a Full Account of the Customs, Commerce, Religion, and Strange Opinions of the Savages of that Country* (London: John Brindley and Charles Corbett, 1735).

This map, taken from the second English edition of Lahontan's book, sketches the route Lahontan purportedly took, and illustrates what was supposedly drawn for him by the Gnacsitare tribe. From an explorer's point of view, the map intriguingly shows a very close connection between the end of the Longue River and the beginning of a large river going west, toward the Pacific. If Lahontan was correct, once a single range of mountains was crossed, expeditions could presumably just float down toward the Pacific.

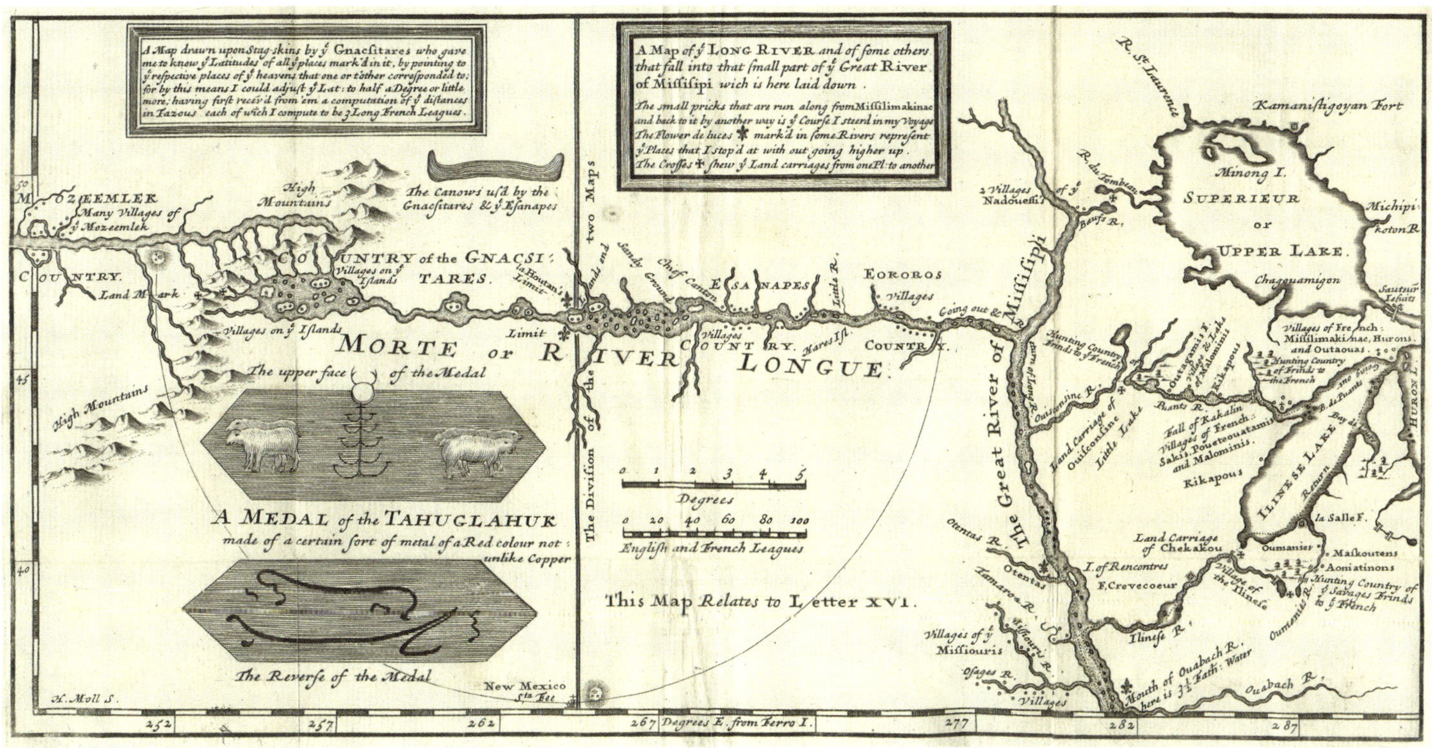

The Indian Fort SASQUESAHANOK
A New MAP of the North Parts of AMERICA claimed by FRANCE under ye Names of LOUISIANA, MISSISIPI, CANADA and NEW FRANCE with ye Adjoyning Territories of ENGLAND and SPAIN.
UPPER LAKE
CANADA
HURON
LAKE Michigane
ILINESE LAKE
NEW FRANCE
LOUISIANA
PARTS UNKNOWN
GREAT TEGUAIO
Apaches de Navaio
APACHERIA COUNTRY
NEW MEXICO
GULF OF CALIFORNIA
PART OF CALIFORNIA
NEW SCOTLAND
NEW FOUND LAND
THE BANKS OF NEW FOUND LAND
VIRGINIA
WESTERN OCEAN
GULF OF MEXICO
BAHAMA ISLANDS
CUBA I.
HISPANIOLA
NORTH SEA
THE GREAT SOUTH SEA
NEW SPAIN
Bay of Campechy
Tropick of Cancer
The Harbour of ANNAPOLIS ROYAL
A Map of ye Mouth of MISSISIPI and MOBILE Rivers &c.
A Scale of English Miles
ADVERTISEMENT
EXPLANATION
Explanation of an Expedition in Florida Neck, by Thirty three Iamasees Indians Accompany'd by Capt T. Nairn.

7

HERMAN MOLL (1654?–1732) · *A NEW MAP OF THE NORTH PARTS OF AMERICA CLAIMED BY FRANCE UNDER YE NAMES OF LOUISIANA, MISSISSIPI, CANADA AND NEW FRANCE WITH YE ADJOYNING TERRITORIES OF ENGLAND AND SPAIN*

Copperplate engraving, 40 x 23¾ in. From: *The World Described, or A New and Correct Set of Maps . . . Engraved in Copper by Herman Moll, Geographer* (London: Herman Moll, 1715–20).

On Moll's map, the source of the Mississippi River was shown at about 109 degrees west longitude, when, in fact it begins at about 95 degrees west longitude, some 650 miles further east than this map showed. The map also has a notation "La Hontan's Limit," showing where the Frenchman purportedly traveled.

8

JOHN SENEX (1678–1740) · *A MAP OF LOUISIANA AND OF THE RIVER MISSISSIPI*

Copperplate engraving, 22½ x 18¾ in. From: *A New General Atlas, Containing a Geographical and Historical Account of All the Empires, Kingdomes and Other Dominions of the World* (London: Daniel Browne, Thomas Taylor, et. al., 1721).

John Senex was an eighteenth-century English map printer and publisher who didn't mind stealing other people's work. This 1721 map is a good example. Senex's map is almost a word-for-word English translation of Guillaume Delisle's map (without attribution to Delisle), including even translating the words of Delisle's description "Indiens Errans et Antropophages" to "Wandering Indians and Maneaters."

A MAP OF LOUISIANA AND OF THE RIVER MISSISSIPI By Iohn Senex
THIS MAP of the MISSISSIPI Is Most humbly Inscribed to William Law of Lauriston Esq.
LOUISIANA
COUNTRY OF THE APACHES AND OF THE PADOUCAS
COUNTRY OF THE OSAGES
ILINOIS
UPPER LAKE
LAKE HURON
L. MICHIGAN
L. ONTARIO
LAKE ERIE OR DU CHAT
IROQUOIS
PART OF CANADA OR NEW FRANCE
MARYLAND
VIRGINIA
CAROLINA
FLORIDA
NEW MEXICO
NEW BISCAY
NEW KINGDOM OF LEON
GULF OF MEXICO
Wandering Indians & Man-eaters
Mouth of the Missisipi or R. St. Louis
Bay St. Louis or St. Bernard
A Scale of Leagues 20 to a Degree
EXPLANATION

⁂ 9 ⁂

JONATHAN CARVER (1710–1780)

[Detail from:] *A NEW MAP OF NORTH AMERICA, FROM THE LATEST DISCOVERIES 1778, ENGRAV'D FOR CARVERS TRAVELS*

Copperplate engraving, 14 x 13 in. From: *Travels Through the Interior Parts of North America in the Years 1766, 1767, and 1768*, third ed. (London: C. Dilly, 1781).

Carver had no idea that there was a "River of the West," but he, like numerous other explorers of the time, not only placed the river squarely across the middle of the North American continent, but placed its source very close to the sources of rivers which ran eastward into the Mississippi River.

10

JONATHAN CARVER (1710–1780)

[Detail from:] *A NEW MAP OF NORTH AMERICA, FROM THE LATEST DISCOVERIES 1778, ENGRAV'D FOR CARVERS TRAVELS*

Copperplate engraving, 14 x 13 in. From: *Travels Through the Interior Parts of North America in the Years 1766, 1767, and 1768*, third ed. (London: C. Dilly, 1781).

This map from the 1781 edition of Carver's book shows what appear to be eleven new states, carved out of the western territories of what would become the United States two years later, in 1783. Thomas Jefferson proposed several states for the area, but only three years after Carver had done so.

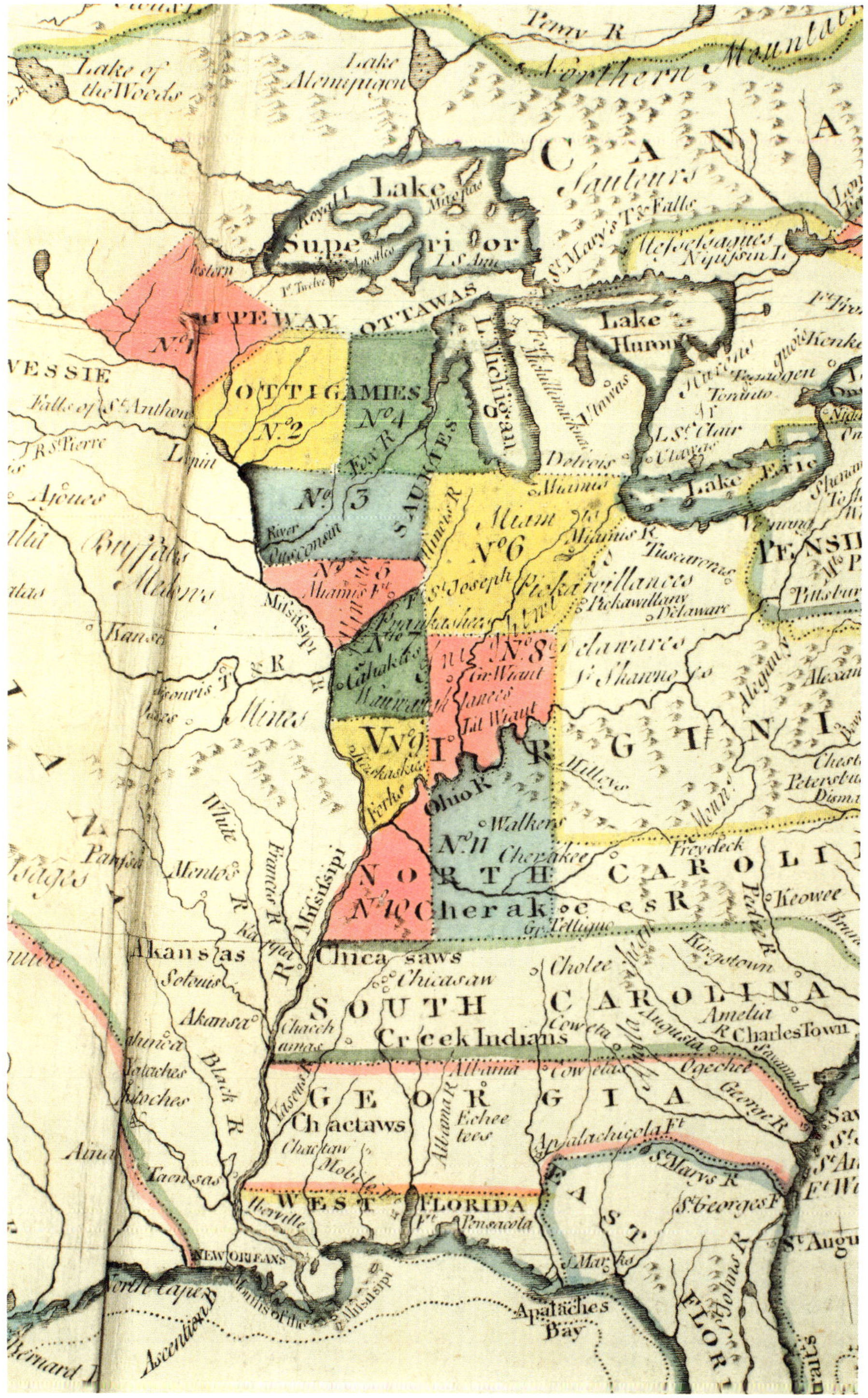

II

EXPLORING BOUNDARIES: THE BRITISH NORTHWEST, THE SPANISH SOUTHWEST AND THE LOUISIANA PURCHASE

ALMOST AS SOON AS the United States became a nation, efforts were undertaken to explore the far west of North America, although it was clear that the then-current western border was the Mississippi River. Four expeditions were commissioned in the 1790s alone. Thomas Jefferson, who served as George Washington's first secretary of state, actively supported three of them. One of the expeditions was a sea voyage up the west coast of North America, commanded by Robert Gray. During that voyage, Gray and his crew discovered a previously unknown river that flowed into the Pacific. Gray named it after his ship, the *Columbia*, thus establishing an American claim to that part of the continent. In another effort, the American Philosophical Society commissioned a young French naturalist, André Michaux, to locate the "shortest & most convenient route of communication between the U. S. and the Pacific Ocean,"[8] utilizing the Missouri River as a part of the route. For political reasons, though, Michaux's expedition never got further west than Kentucky.

Just as the launch of *Sputnik* in the late 1950s galvanized America to enter the space race, the publication of Alexander Mackenzie's book *Voyages from Montreal, on the River St. Laurence, Through the Continent of North America, to the Frozen and Pacific Oceans; in the Years 1789 and 1793* (London, 1801) galvanized then-president Jefferson to ask Congress to commission an overland expedition to the Pacific by the United States. Mackenzie, a British employee of the North West Company, one of the two British North American fur trapping and trading concessions (the other was the Hudson's Bay Company), sought to traverse what is now Canada to the Pacific Ocean. After a failed attempt, in which he ended up at the Arctic Ocean, he succeeded in 1793, describing his travels in *Voyages from Montreal* (fig. 11). Jefferson obtained a copy of this book, and he and Meriwether Lewis, his secretary, studied its text and map. At that point, even before the Louisiana Purchase in 1803, Lewis began to be groomed to lead an expedition to the Pacific.

Another map of the West consulted by Jefferson and Lewis before the Lewis and Clark expedition of 1804–06 was an 1802 map by Aaron Arrowsmith, an English map publisher. No Americans had ever reached as far as the Great Bend of the Missouri River prior to the Lewis and Clark ex-

8. www.monticello.org/site/jefferson/jeffersons-instructions-to-michaux (accessed July 23, 2017).

pedition, but some French and English fur traders had, and had mapped up to that point, in a general way. However, Jefferson and Lewis had no idea what the western part of the Missouri River basin was going to look like. Arrowsmith, though, had the benefit of some mapping done by fur trappers and traders of the Hudson's Bay Company. One of those individuals, Peter Fidler, had transcribed some maps provided to him by a Blackfoot Indian named Ah ko mo ki ("The Feathers"). On his 1802 map of North America, Arrowsmith inserted a series of dotted lines west from the Great Bend of the Missouri to the Rocky Mountains, based on Fidler's sketches of Ah ko mo ki's rendition of the western river system. As it turned out, these dotted lines provided a remarkably accurate portrayal of the western Missouri River area, and Lewis and Clark benefitted enormously from this information.

In 1804, Arrowsmith and Samuel Lewis, a Philadelphia mapmaker, teamed up to produce a world atlas. Four of the maps in that atlas dealt with the American West, including a reduced-size version of Arrowsmith's 1802 map, *North America*. Though the dotted lines of Ah ko mo ki turned out to be correct (fig. 12), a number of other topographical assumptions on some of the maps were wrong. For example, several maps showed only a single range of mountains between Canada and the Southwest when, in fact, there were multiple ranges. In addition, one of the four maps, *British Possessions in North America*, based in large part on Mackenzie's explorations across Canada in 1793, showed the Columbia River arising in western Canada and flowing south, and then west, into the Pacific. Mackenzie (and Arrowsmith and Lewis) had called this river system the "Tacoutche Tesse or Columbia River." In fact, the river that Mackenzie erroneously thought was the source of the Columbia was the Fraser River (fig. 13). Though the maps here illustrated are from an 1812 Arrowsmith and Lewis atlas, the maps are identical to the 1802 and 1804 maps.

Although it is little remembered today, Thomas Jefferson commissioned three explorations of portions of the Louisiana Purchase territory. The best known, of course, was that of Meriwether Lewis and William Clark, across what became the northwest part of the United States. However, Jefferson also sent out two other parties to explore the southwestern reaches of the Purchase. One was a party headed up by Thomas Freeman and Peter Curtis, in 1806, to map the Red River (the arguable western boundary of the Purchase) to its sources. However, Freeman and Curtis were turned back by the Spanish. The other was a party headed by Dr. George Hunter and William Dunbar, who explored the Washita River, into central Arkansas, in 1804 and early 1805. When that party returned, Nicholas King, the first surveyor of the city of Washington, DC, drew a map for Jefferson, using data brought back to him from the expedition. Since the US Government Printing Office had not yet been established, the map was privately engraved and printed in Philadelphia, and very few copies were printed. The map shown here is a 1904 re-strike from the original 1806 copperplate (fig. 14).

The Lewis and Clark expedition, on the other hand, was widely publicized and has long been well known in the annals of exploration of the American West. Lewis and Clark were not trying to cross territory claimed by Spain or, for that matter, by anyone except Native Americans. The British may have had some fur traders and trappers in the Pacific Northwest, but not enough to interfere with Lewis and Clark. Most of us have probably learned something about the Lewis and Clark expedition in our history and geography classes: that it began in St. Louis and continued to the Pacific and back in the early years of the nineteenth century; that a Native American woman, Sacajawea, and her baby went along; and that the difficulty of crossing the continent became very apparent upon the return of Lewis and Clark's Corps of Discovery. However, much information about the expedition is less well-known: that eight years elapsed between the end of the explorations and the publication of the reports and maps; that Meriwether

Lewis was accused of financial irregularities and committed suicide in 1809; and that the large map of the expedition, though incorrect in a number of particulars, became the standard against which all mapping of the Pacific Northwest was measured during the first half of the nineteenth century (fig. 15). The fact of the matter remains that Lewis and Clark were the first citizens of the new United States to follow the Missouri River to its sources; the first to follow the Columbia River from several of its sources to its mouth; and the first to establish good relations with dozens of Native American tribes, without whose help it would have been much more difficult to settle the West. All of this was achieved with the loss of only one person on the trip, probably from a case of appendicitis.

Even though the official report and maps from the Lewis and Clark expedition were not published until 1814, stories of their journey circulated long before then. A member of the Lewis and Clark party, Patrick Gass, even published his own description of the trip. In 1809, only three years after the conclusion of the expedition, an unauthorized version of Lewis & Clark's journey appeared in print in England. It contained a truncated history of the expedition; the 1806 letter from Jefferson to Congress describing the expedition; an 1806 letter about the trip from William Clark to his brother; a description of Hunter and Dunbar's trip into Central Arkansas; and other miscellany. Significantly, that book also contained one of the first published maps of the far West which showed topographical features (such as rivers) named by Lewis and Clark, and Fort Clatsop, the Corps of Discovery's winter quarters on the Pacific (fig. 16).

In spite of the inability of Jefferson's expeditions to cross into the Southwest, much exploration and mapping were done in the early years of the nineteenth century. Prussian polymath Alexander von Humboldt (known, when he lived in France, as Alexander de Humboldt) traveled extensively in Latin America, observing and writing about the flora and fauna he found there, and about the political and cultural climate (fig. 17). Importantly for Western exploration, he spent several months in Mexico City in 1804, consulting reports and maps by Spanish explorers of the American Southwest, and prepared an up-to-date-map of the Southwest. His map was called the most accurate published as of that time by map historian Carl Wheat.[9] It correctly showed the Gila River emptying into the Colorado, above the Gulf of California; it accurately portrayed the Cordilleras Mountains of New Mexico connecting with the central Rockies further north; and it proposed that the Nepeste River of the Spanish southwest and the Arkansas River in the Midwest were probably the same river.

However, Humboldt's map also perpetuated some myths. It showed a Rio de S. Buenaventura flowing into a large salt lake, and also stated that some historians believed the Aztecs migrated from a large Lake Timpanogos (or Lake Teguayo) area of what is now Utah, to the Valley of Mexico, by way of Casa Grande, Arizona (fig. 18). By the time Humboldt's map was published in 1811, a number of others had published maps containing very similar information. These included American explorer Zebulon Pike and British cartographer Aaron Arrowsmith. Humboldt was quite annoyed at this development, but he had left a copy of the manuscript of this map at the State Department in Washington in 1804, and it is thought that a number of people may have made copies.

---

9. Carl I. Wheat, *Mapping the Transmississippi West, Vol. One – The Spanish Entrada to the Louisiana Purchase 1540–1804* (Mansfield Centre CT: Martino Publishing, 2004), 136–7

At about the same time Lewis and Clark were returning from their journey, Army lieutenant Zebulon Montgomery Pike was heading west, pursuant to orders from General James Wilkinson, the governor of the Louisiana Territory, to locate and map the headwaters of the "Arkansaw" and Red Rivers. Wilkinson, who was a close associate of Aaron Burr, was a true scoundrel and, at the very least, an informant to the Spanish regarding American troop movements. What role, if any, Pike had in Wilkinson's and Burr's schemes is not known. However, Pike's mission—to discover the sources of the Red River—had been one of Jefferson's goals after the Louisiana Purchase. The only description of what the United States received from the 1803 Louisiana Purchase was that it got what France had gotten from Spain in 1800. (France had claimed that territory from 1699 until 1762, when it ceded it to Spain, and Napoleon got it back from Spain in 1800.) Many Americans believed the southwestern boundary of the Louisiana Purchase was the Red River, and Jefferson wanted that area explored. However, the Spanish did not agree with that interpretation, and they had already intercepted one of Jefferson's expeditions and sent it packing.

When Pike went west, he managed to elude the Spanish long enough to get to present-day Pueblo, Colorado; discover and identify what he claimed, incorrectly, was the highest peak in the Rocky Mountains (now known as Pike's Peak); and explore the Sangre de Cristo Mountains and the San Luis Valley of Colorado. Ultimately, he and his companions were captured by the Spanish, sent to Mexico and deported back to the United States. Pike was killed in the War of 1812.

Though much of Pike's mapping was lost, he was able to reconstruct much of that work, and his mapping of the territories of what are now Colorado and New Mexico was used for years by those going west. Pike disparaged much of the land he explored as not fit for settlement, and that attitude, reiterated by others, discouraged settlement in that part of the West for several decades. His account of his travels, along with several maps, were published several years before Lewis and Clark's reports (fig. 19).

11

ALEXANDER MACKENZIE (1764–1820) · *VOYAGES FROM MONTREAL, ON THE RIVER ST. LAURENCE, THROUGH THE CONTINENT OF NORTH AMERICA, TO THE FROZEN AND PACIFIC OCEANS; IN THE YEARS 1789 AND 1793*

London: T. Cadell, Jun. and W. Davies; Cobbett and Morgan; and Edinburgh: W. Creech, 1802.

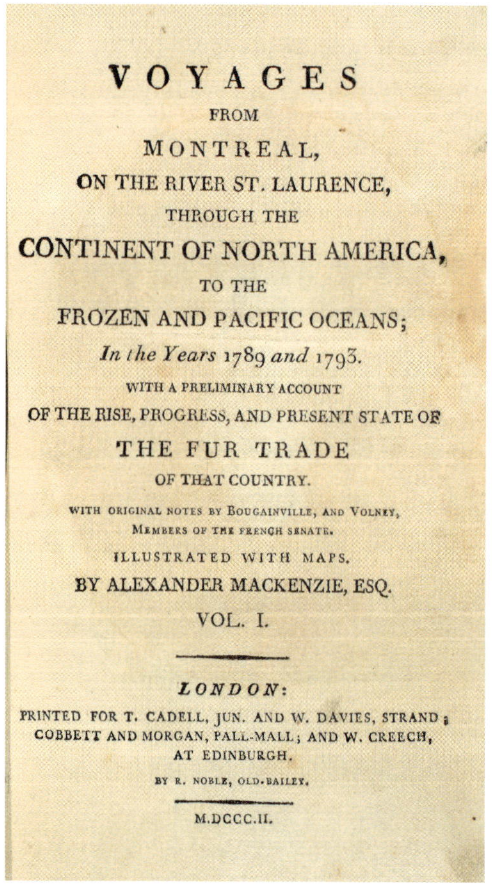

VOYAGES
FROM
MONTREAL,
ON THE RIVER ST. LAURENCE,
THROUGH THE
CONTINENT OF NORTH AMERICA,
TO THE
FROZEN AND PACIFIC OCEANS;
In the Years 1789 *and* 1793.
WITH A PRELIMINARY ACCOUNT
OF THE RISE, PROGRESS, AND PRESENT STATE OF
THE FUR TRADE
OF THAT COUNTRY.
WITH ORIGINAL NOTES BY BOUGAINVILLE, AND VOLNEY,
MEMBERS OF THE FRENCH SENATE.
ILLUSTRATED WITH MAPS.
BY ALEXANDER MACKENZIE, ESQ.
VOL. I.

LONDON:
PRINTED FOR T. CADELL, JUN. AND W. DAVIES, STRAND; COBBETT AND MORGAN, PALL-MALL; AND W. CREECH, AT EDINBURGH.
BY R. NOBLE, OLD-BAILEY.
M.DCCC.II.

Mackenzie attempted to cross the North American continent twice. In 1789, he made a wrong turn and ended up at the Arctic Ocean, but in 1793, he made it all the way across. Thomas Jefferson and Meriwether Lewis were familiar with his report and map before the Lewis and Clark expedition. Many think Jefferson planned Lewis's expedition, even before the Louisiana Purchase, to contest Mackenzie's claims on behalf of the British crown.

12

AARON ARROWSMITH (1750–1823) AND SAMUEL LEWIS (D. 1822)

Detail from: *NORTH AMERICA*

Philadelphia: Arrowsmith & Lewis, 1804. Copperplate engraving, 8¾ x 10¾ in., drawn By Samuel Lewis, engraved by Benjamin Tanner. From: *A New and Elegant General Atlas, Comprising All the New Discoveries, to the Present Time* (Boston: Thomas & Andrews, 1812).

In 1801, Peter Fidler, a Hudson's Bay Company surveyor, saw a map of the river system west of the Great Bend of the Missouri River that had been prepared by a Blackfoot Indian named Ah ko mo ki ("The Feathers"). He re-drew that map and submitted it to his employer. The map was made known to English geographer, mapmaker and publisher Aaron Arrowsmith through his contacts at the Hudson's Bay Company, and Arrowsmith incorporated the western reaches of the Missouri River into a map he prepared in 1802. He showed the western reaches of the Missouri as dotted lines to indicate that he was not sure they were correct.

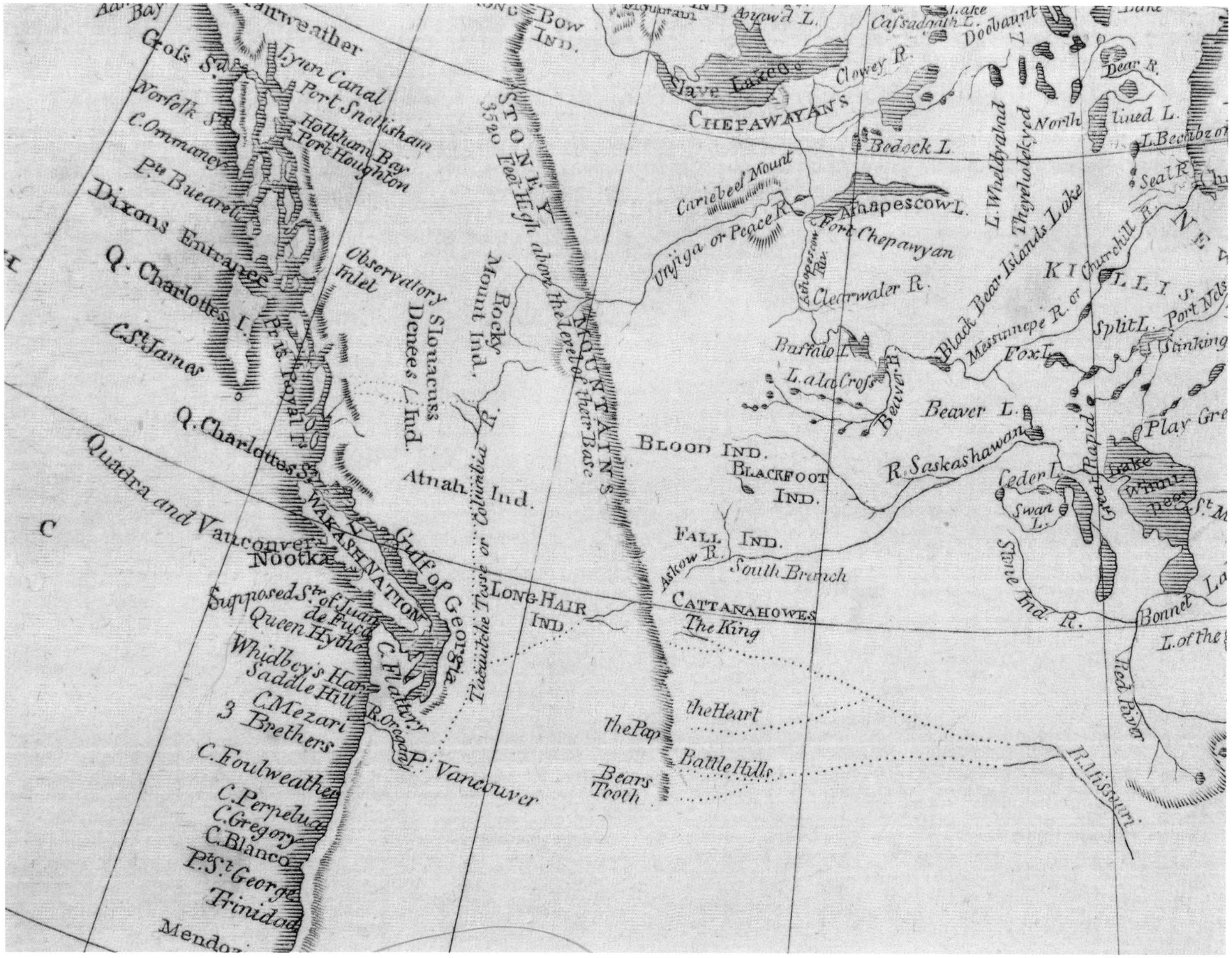

Lynn Canal
Port Snettisham
Norfolk Sd.
C. Ommaney
Port Houghton
Pto. Bucareli
Dixons Entrance
Q. Charlottes I.
C. St. James
Observatory Inlet
Slouacuss Denees Ind.
Rocky Mount Ind.
BOW IND.
STONEY
3520 Feet High above the Level of their Base
MOUNTAINS
Slave Lake
CHEPAWAYANS
Clowey R.
Dear R.
Bedock L.
Caribeef Mount
Athapescow L.
Unjiga or Peace R.
Fort Chepawyan
Clearwater R.
Buffalo L.
L. a la Cross
Beaver R.
Black Bear Islands Lake
Missinnepe R. or Churchill R.
Fox L.
Split L.
Beaver L.
R. Saskashawan
Ceder L.
Swan L.
Great Rapid
Atnah Ind.
BLOOD IND.
BLACKFOOT IND.
FALL IND.
Askow R.
South Branch
Stone Ind. R.
Q. Charlottes Sd.
Quadra and Vancouver
Nootka
WAKASH NATION
Gulf of Georgia
LONG HAIR IND.
CATTANAHOWES
The King
Supposed Str. of Juan de Fuca
Queen Hythe
Whidbey's Har.
Saddle Hill
C. Mezari
3 Brethers
C. Flattery
R. Oregan
P. Vancouver
Tacoutche Tesse or Columbia R.
the Heart
the Pap
Battle Hills
Bears Tooth
C. Foulweather
C. Perpelua
C. Gregory
C. Blanco
Pt. St. George
Trinidad
Bonnet
Red River
R. Missouri

13

AARON ARROWSMITH (1750–1823) AND SAMUEL LEWIS (D. 1822)

[Detail from:] *BRITISH POSSESSIONS IN AMERICA*

Philadelphia: Arrowsmith & Lewis, 1804. Copperplate engraving, 8¾ x 10¾ in., drawn By Samuel Lewis, engraved by Benjamin Tanner.
From: *A New and Elegant General Atlas, Comprising All the New Discoveries, to the Present Time* (Boston: Thomas & Andrews, 1812).

This map once again showed the western Missouri River as Ah ko mo ki had sketched it. This time, however, three landmark mountain formations drawn in by the Blackfoot were illustrated: the "King," the "Heart" and "Bear's Teeth." Though the "King" is now called Chief Mountain, all of these landmarks were located and identified by Lewis and Clark, and others, on the way west. The map also shows Mackenzie's erroneous belief regarding the source of the Columbia River.

14

WILLIAM DUNBAR (1750–1810) AND NICHOLAS KING (1771–1812)
MAP OF THE WASHITA RIVER IN LOUISIANA FROM THE HOT SPRINGS TO THE CONFLUENCE OF THE RED RIVER WITH THE MISSISSIPPI

Boston: Houghton, Mifflin & Co., 1904. 33¼ x 8 in.

Nicholas King was an English-born and trained surveyor who came to the United States in 1794. In the mid-1790s, he moved to the site of the new capital, and surveyed land there, and in 1802, he became the official surveyor for the District of Columbia. He drew numerous maps at Thomas Jefferson's request and first drew this map in 1806. In 1904, a photolithograph was made from the original copper plate engraving in the War Department, and 550 copies were made. Most were bound into *Documents Relating to the Purchase and Exploration of Louisiana*, 2 vols., (Boston: Houghton, Mifflin, 1904). However, this copy appears never to have been folded into a book.

15

WILLIAM CLARK (1770–1838)

A MAP OF LEWIS AND CLARK'S TRACK ACROSS THE WESTERN PORTION OF NORTH AMERICA, FROM THE MISSISSIPPI TO THE PACIFIC OCEAN, BY ORDER OF THE EXECUTIVE OF THE UNITED STATES IN 1804, 5 & 6

Copperplate engraving, 27 x 11¾ in. From: *Travels to the Source of the Missouri River and Across the American Continent to the Pacific Ocean Performed by Order of the Government of the United States In the Years 1804, 1805 and 1806 by Captains Lewis and Clark* (London: Longman, Hurst, Rees, Orme & Brown, 1814).

This map, published both in Philadelphia and in London in 1814, is one of the seminal maps in American history. It was the first to lay out the region of the continent that later became the northwestern United States with any degree of accuracy. The text that accompanied the map described Lewis and Clark's journey in great detail for others to follow.

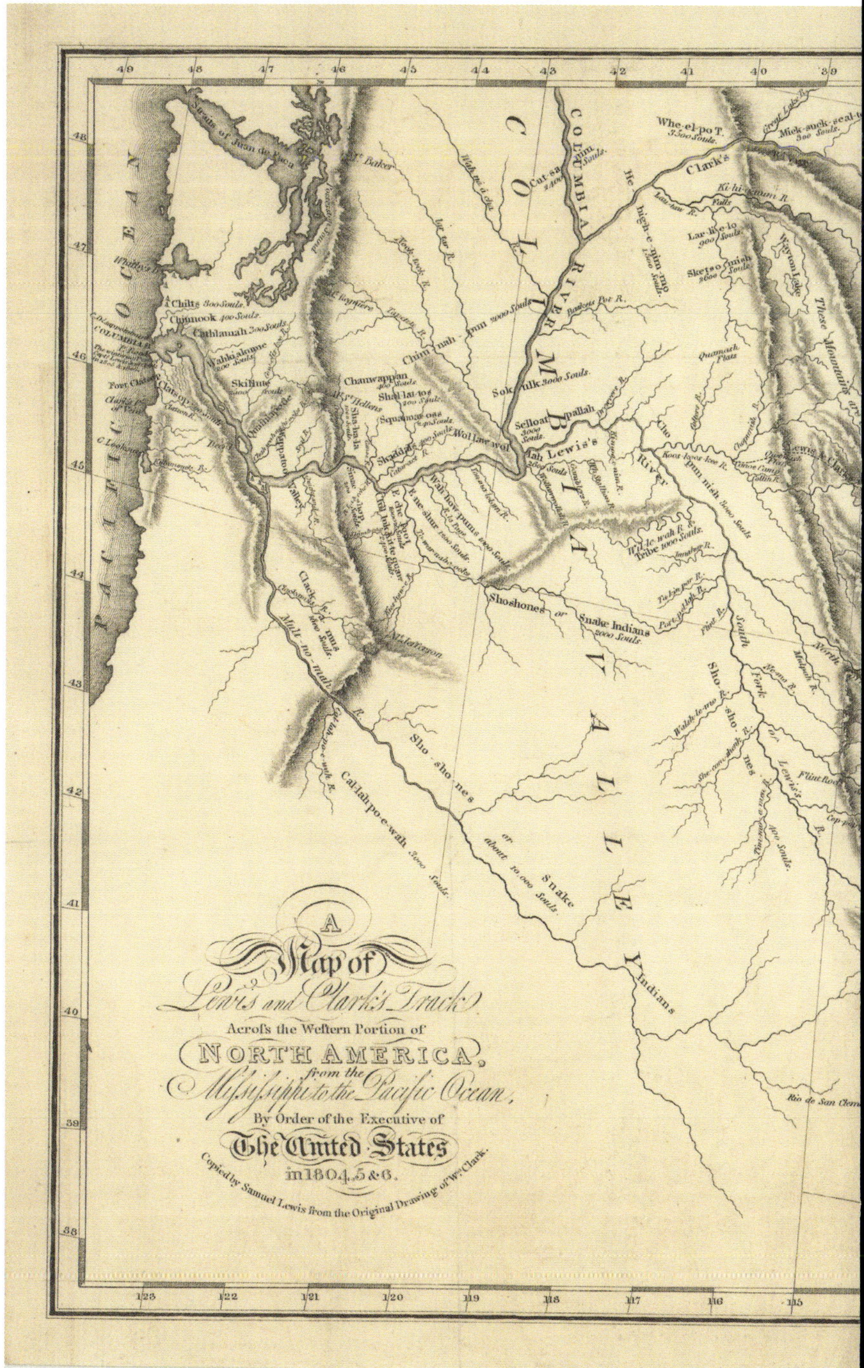

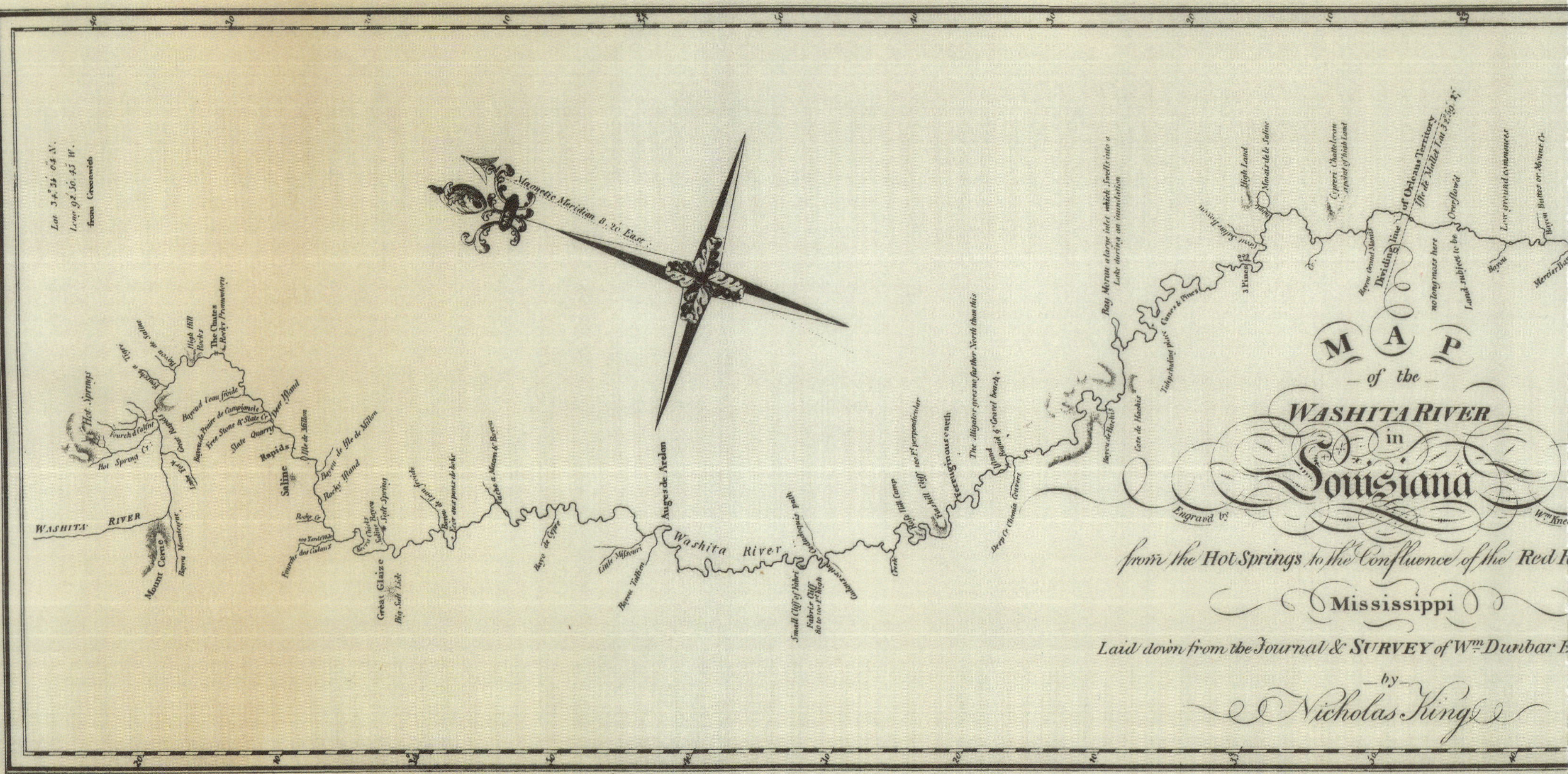
MAP
of the
WASHITA RIVER
in
Louisiana
Mississippi
Laid down from the Journal & SURVEY of Wm. Dunbar
by
Nicholas King
Magnetic Meridian 8. 26 East
Hot Springs
Hot Spring Cr.
WASHITA RIVER
Washita River
Mount Cerne
Saline
Rapids
Deer Island
Great Glaize
Big Salt Lick
Augres de Ardon
Little Missouri
Ferruginous earth
Dividing line of Orleans Territory
Low ground commences

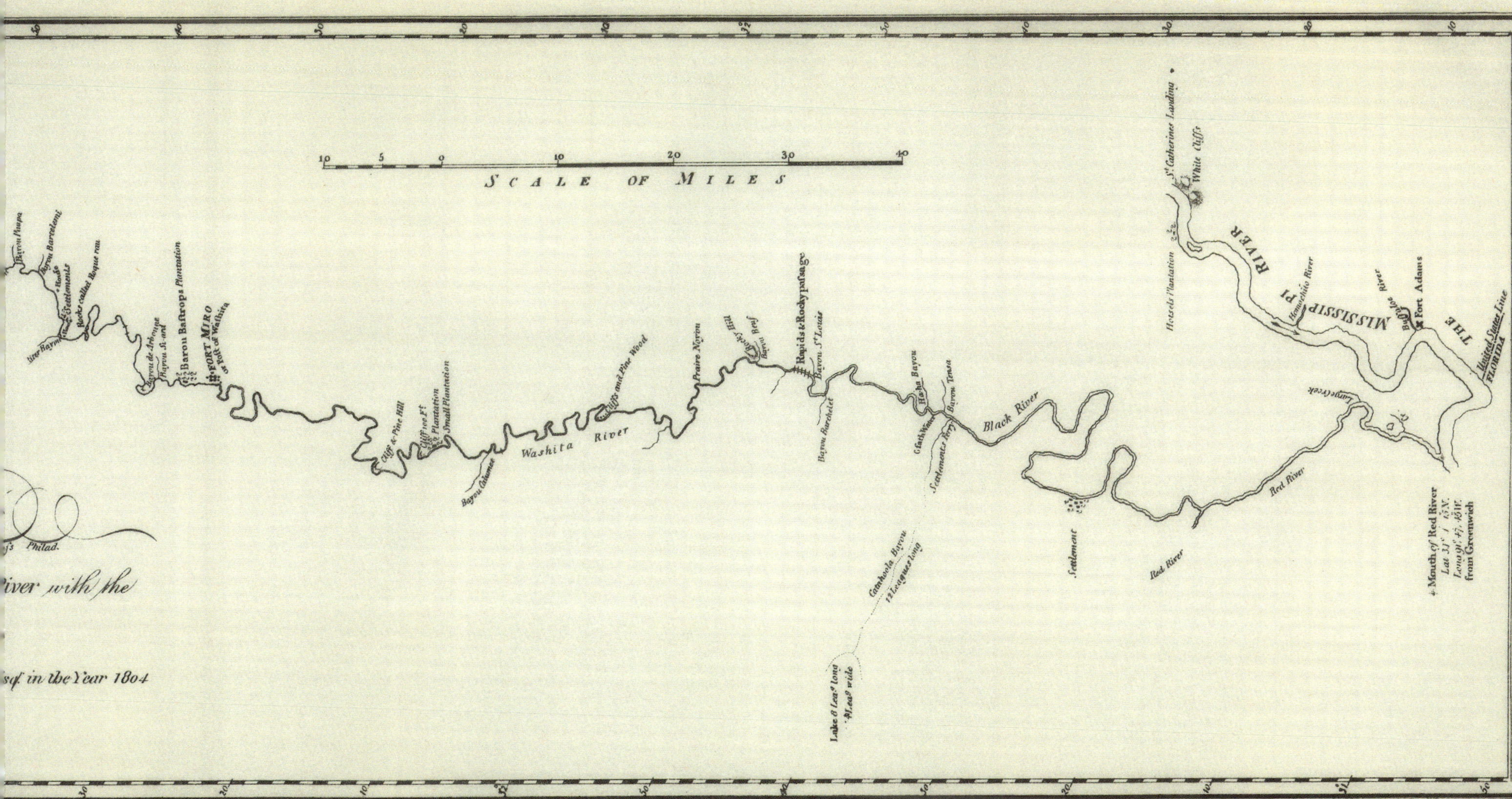

SCALE OF MILES
Washita River
Black River
Red River
MISSISSIPPI RIVER
Fort Adams
St Catherines Landing
White Cliffs
THE
United States Line
FLORIDA
Mouth of Red River
Lat 31° 1' 15" N.
Long 91° 47' 45" W.
from Greenwich
Baron Bastrop's Plantation
FORT MIRO
or Post of Washita
Bayou de Arbonne
Bayou Siard
Rapids & Rocky passage
Bayou St Louis
Cliffs and Pine Wood
Cliff & Pine Hill
Plantation
Small Plantation
Bayou Tensa
Settlements Ferry
Settlement
Catahoola Bayou
12 Leagues long
Philad.
iver with the
in the Year 1804

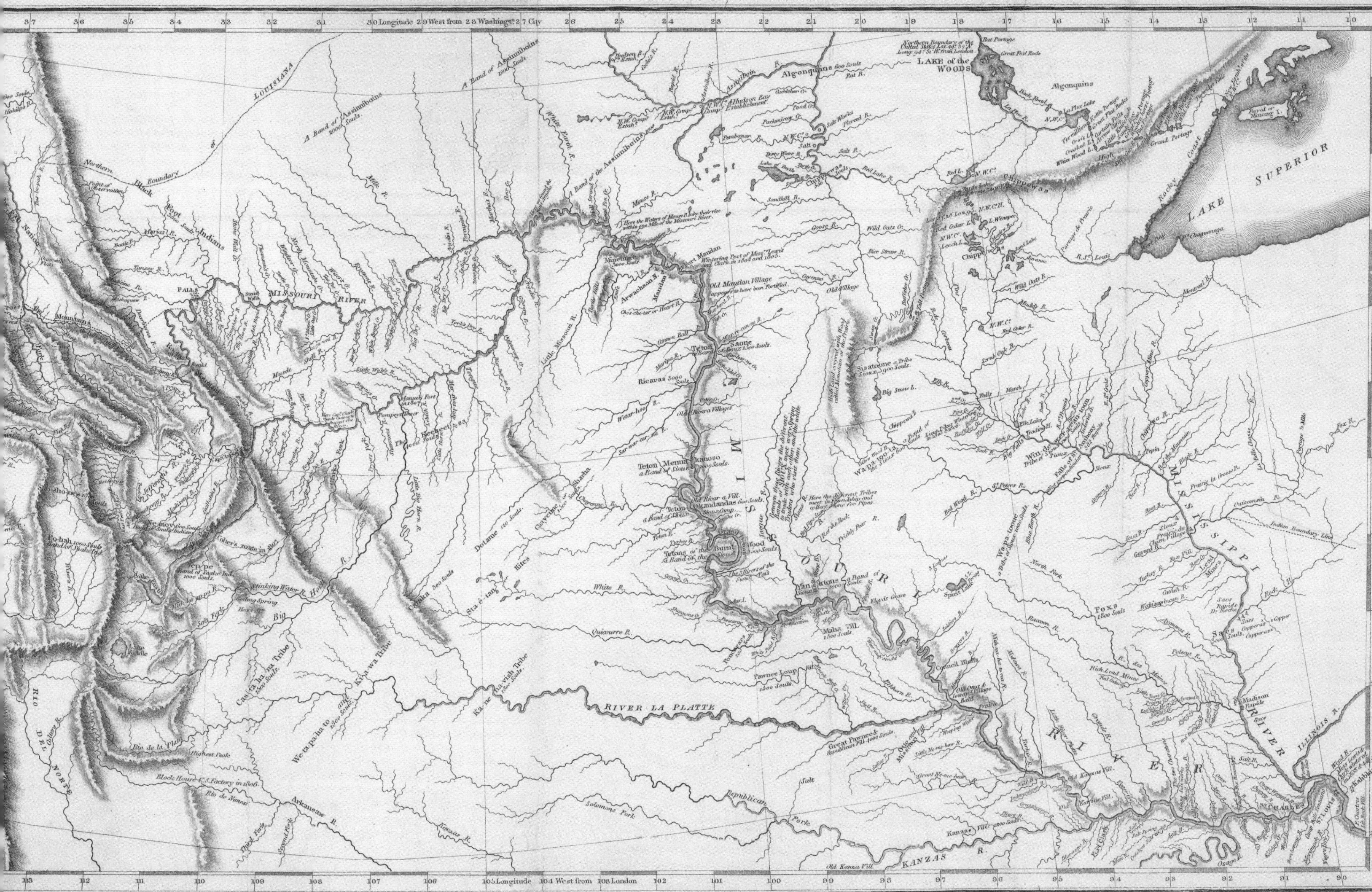

London Published April 28th 1814 by Longman, Hurst, Rees, Orme, & Brown, Paternoster Row.

16

[Detail from:] *MAP OF THE COUNTRY INHABITED BY THE WESTERN TRIBES OF INDIANS*

London: Longman & Co., 1809. Copperplate engraving, 9½ x 7¾ in. From: *The Travels of Capts. Lewis & Clarke* [sic], *from St. Louis, by Way of the Missouri, and Columbia Rivers, to the Pacific Ocean; Performed in the Years 1804, 1805, & 1806, by Order of the Government of the United States* (London: Longman, Hurst, Rees, and Orme, 1809).

Though this map contained a number of inaccuracies (probably because it was based on written descriptions of the trip, rather than actual cartography), it is one of the earliest known images to show, and name, several topographical features of the western half of the Lewis & Clark expedition to the Pacific. In addition, it identifies Fort Clatsop, Lewis and Clark's quarters in the winter of 1805–06. The official Lewis and Clark map that included the western part of their journey would not be published until 1814.

17

ALEXANDER DE HUMBOLDT (1769–1859) *POLITICAL ESSAY ON THE KINGDOM OF NEW SPAIN*, VOLS. 1–4

London: Longman, Hurst, Rees, Orme, and Brown, 1811.

The Prussian naturalist Alexander de Humboldt summarized his journeys throughout South America, Central America, and New Spain (part of which is the present southwest United States) in this multi-volume work translated from the French edition published in Paris the same year (*Essai politique sur le royaume de la Nouvelle-Espagne*).

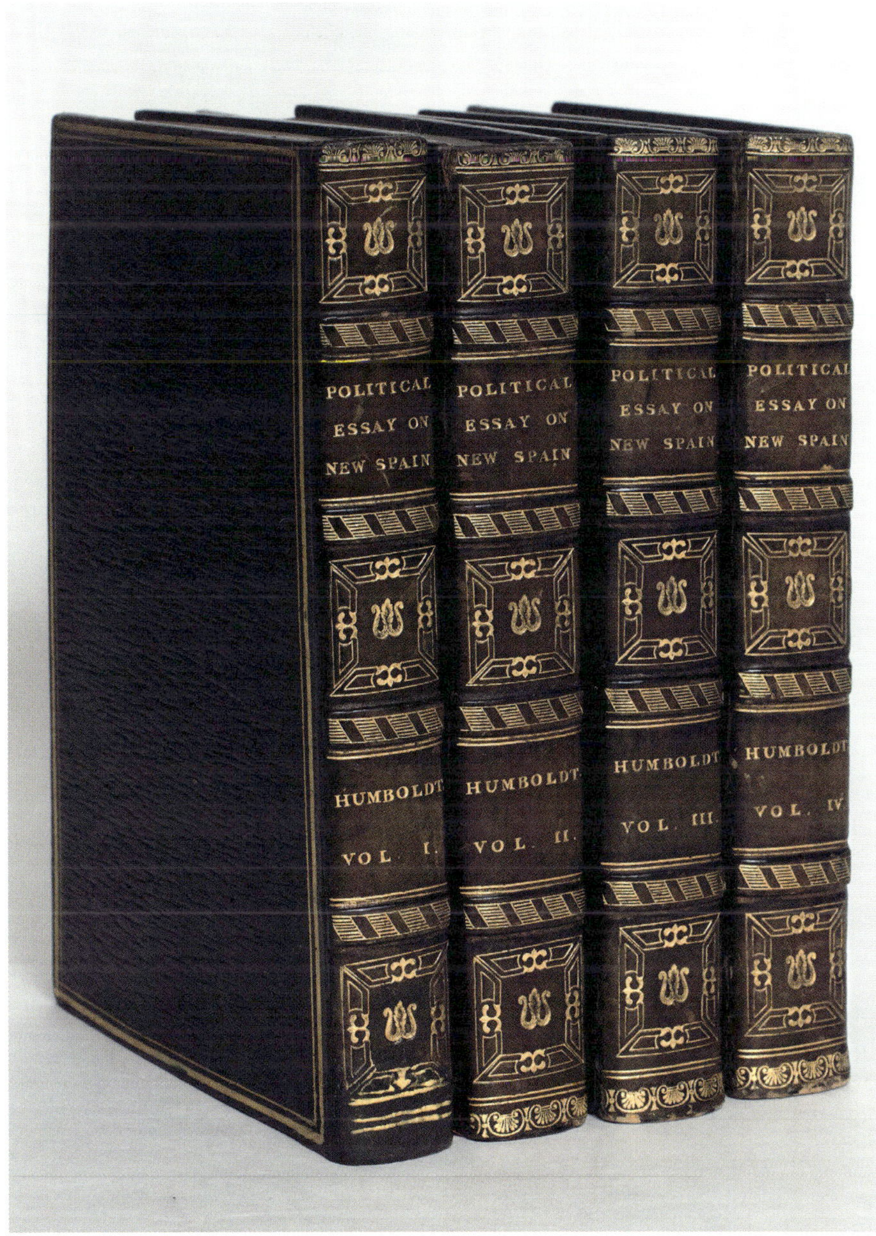

A MAP OF
NEW SPAIN
from 16°. to 38°. North Latitude
reduced from the Large Map drawn from
astronomical observations at Mexico
in the Year 1804,
BY ALEXANDRE DE HUMBOLDT,
and comprehending the whole of the information contained in the
Original Map,
except the heights of the Mountains.
Longitude West from Greenwich
LOUISIANA
belonging to the United States
NEW MEXICO
SANTA-FE
Rio Colorado
Rio Gila
Apaches Lipanes Ind.
Apaches Llaneros Ind.
Fertile Savannahs
R. Missouri

18

ALEXANDER DE HUMBOLDT (1769–1859)

[Detail from:] *A MAP OF NEW SPAIN FROM 16° TO 38° NORTH LATITUDE REDUCED FROM THE LARGE MAP DRAWN FROM ASTRONOMICAL OBSERVATIONS AT MEXICO IN THE YEAR 1804, . . . AND COMPREHENDING THE WHOLE OF THE INFORMATION CONTAINED IN THE ORIGINAL MAP, EXCEPT THE HEIGHTS OF THE MOUNTAINS*

Copperplate engraving, 16½ x 11½ in. From: *Political Essay on the Kingdom of New Spain* (London: Longman, Hurst, Rees, Orme, and Brown, 1811).

Humboldt's map, published in a large format, in French, in 1811, and in the smaller format shown here, in English, that same year, covered an area from Nachitoches, in present-day Louisiana, to the Gulf of California, and from a lake called Lake Timpanogos in the north (now known as Utah Lake), to southern Mexico.

19

ZEBULON MONTGOMERY PIKE (1779–1813)
A CHART OF THE INTERNAL PART OF LOUISIANA, INCLUDING ALL THE HITHERTO UNEXPLORED COUNTRIES, LYING BETWEEN THE RIVER LA PLATTE OF THE MISSOURI ON THE N; AND THE RED RIVER ON THE S; THE MISSISSIPPI EAST AND THE MOUNTAINS OF MEXICO WEST; WITH A PART OF NEW MEXICO AND THE PROVINCE OF TEXAS BY Z. M. PIKE CAPTN. U. S. A.

15 x 17 in. From: *An Account of Expeditions to the Sources of the Mississippi, and Through the Western Parts of Louisiana, to the Sources of the Arkansaw, Kans, La Platte, and Pierre Jaun, Rivers; Performed by the Order of the Government of the United States During the Years 1805, 1806, and 1807, and a Tour Through the Interior Parts of New Spain* (Philadelphia: C. & A. Conrad & Co., 1810).

Zebulon Pike was ordered to explore the sources of the Arkansas River and the Red River of Texas in 1806 and 1807. However, Thomas Jefferson didn't issue the order—General James Wilkinson, the governor of the Louisiana Territory, did. Though it is possible Wilkinson genuinely wanted data on what he thought the southwestern boundary of the Louisiana Purchase really was, he was being paid by the Spanish at that time, so no one really knows what his motives were. Pike did not identify the sources of either the Arkansas or the Red; he was captured, imprisoned and deported to the United States by the Spanish, and his journals and maps were confiscated. However, he did discover what would become Pike's Peak and accurately mapped much of the Southwest (from memory, and probably with the help of an 1804 manuscript map Alexander de Humboldt left in Washington).

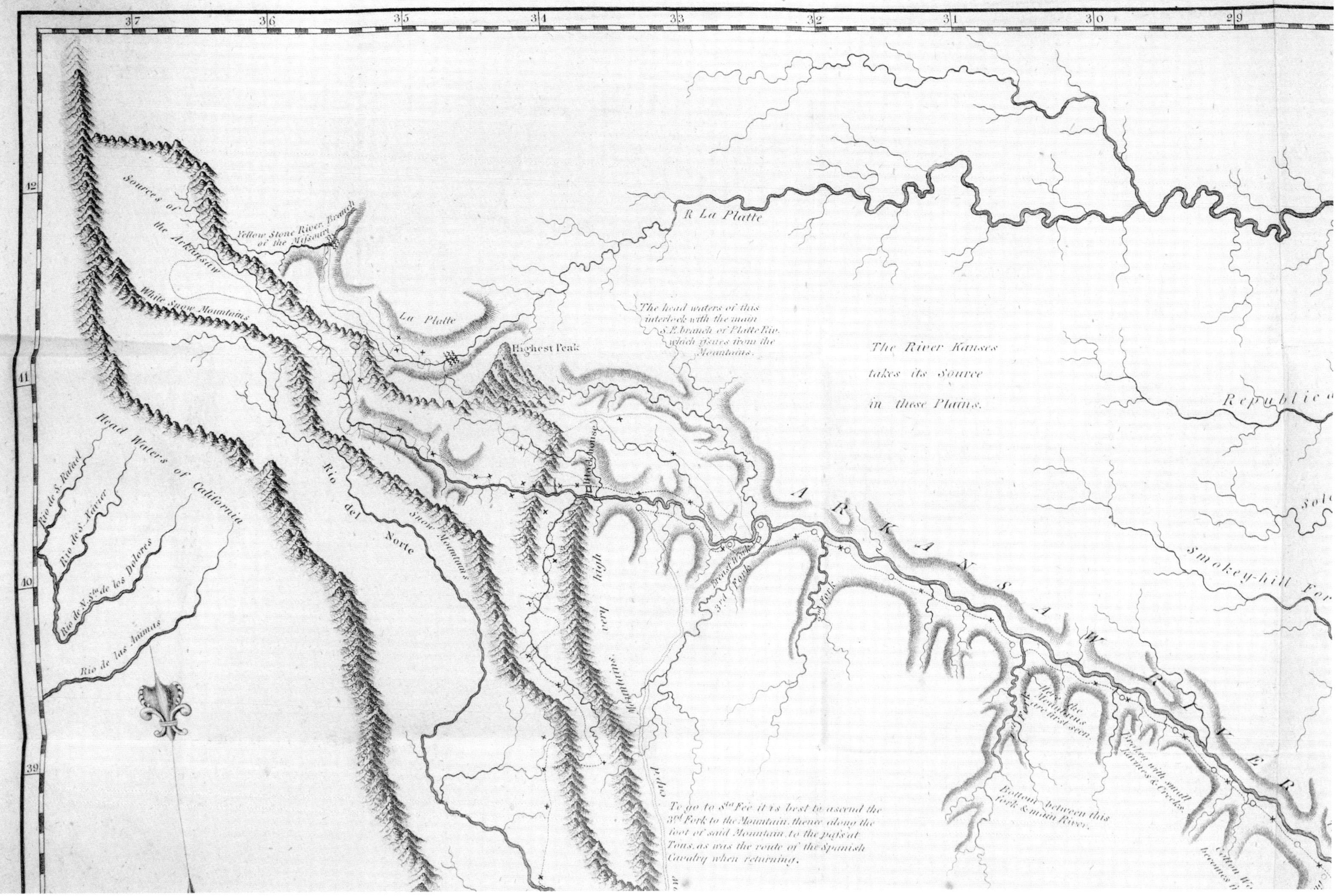
37
36
35
34
33
32
31
30
29
42
41
40
39
Sources of the Arkansaw
Yellow Stone River Branch of the Missouri
White Snow Mountains
La Platte
Highest Peak
R La Platte
The head waters of this interlock with the main S.E. branch of Platte Riv. which issues from the Mountains.
The River Kanses takes its Source in these Plains.
Head Waters of California
Rio del Norte
Snow Mountains
Rio de S. Rafael
Rio de S. Xavier
Rio de las Animas
A R K A N S A W R I V E R
Smokey-hill For
To go to S.ta Fee it is best to ascend the 3rd Fork to the Mountain, thence along the foot of said Mountain to the pass at Tous, as was the route of the Spanish Cavalry when returning.
Bottom between this fork & main River.
Here the Mountains were first seen.

III

EXPLORING AND MAPPING THE WEST: THE US ARMY TAKES THE FIELD

THE US ARMY IN EARLY WESTERN EXPLORATION

The Lewis and Clark expedition was, in actuality, a military undertaking, though President Jefferson and Congress commissioned it, rather than military commanders. Similarly, the Pike mission was a military operation, though it had been organized and put into the field by General Wilkinson, the governor of the Louisiana Territory, rather than senior federal officials in Washington. This individualized approach began to change shortly after the War of 1812, when the US Army began the decades-long tasks of exploring, mapping, fortifying and patrolling the West.

Although many of the US Army's operational units were involved in exploration and mapping, one extremely small group had an outsized involvement: the Corps of Topographical Engineers. Geographers and surveyors were first appointed to military posts during the Revolutionary War to provide information to the troops regarding the terrain through which they would be passing and in which they would be fighting, but their services were no longer required after the war. During the War of 1812, a small unit of topographical engineers was reconstituted. After the war, it was again disbanded. Finally, in 1817, a unit of ten topographical engineers was organized for the initial purpose of mapping locations for the installation of forts. However, it wasn't long before the corps was expanded and other forms of surveying and mapping were incorporated into its duties. The Corps of Topographical Engineers existed until 1863, when it was merged into the much larger Army Corps of Engineers that operates to this day.

Stephen Harriman Long was one of the early members of the Corps of Topographical Engineers. Long, who had begun his career teaching mathematics at West Point, was first assigned to survey inland frontier defenses, from Minnesota to Arkansas. In 1819, he was assigned to trace the sources of the Arkansas River and the Red River in Texas. Efforts had been made to explore the Red River shortly after the Louisiana Purchase, but the river had become increasingly important because under the Adams-Onis Treaty of 1819, Spain and the United States had agreed that it would form a major part of the boundary line between the United States and Spain's territorial possessions.

Long and his party, which included a botanist, a geologist, an entomologist and an artist, went up the Platte River until they sighted the Rocky Mountains. They located a large mountain, which they named Long's Peak. In addition, two of the party climbed what would later be named Pike's

Peak. The party then traveled across country from the Platte to the Arkansas Rivers, exploring what would become Denver and Colorado Springs. They then split up, with part of the group going down the Arkansas River, and the others going south, to look for the sources of the Red River. They thought they found the Red, but when it turned out that the river emptied into the Arkansas River, Long concluded it was the Canadian River instead.

The expedition was not a great success, as several members deserted; journals and notebooks were stolen; food ran short; horses were eaten; hostile Native Americans were encountered; and the sources of neither the Arkansas nor the Red Rivers were discovered. In addition, Long, in his report and map, perpetuated the idea of a "Great Desert" in that part of the West, even labeling it as such on his map (fig. 20). (The so-called Great Desert of Long encompassed parts of present-day Nebraska, Kansas, eastern Colorado, New Mexico and west Texas.) However, the expedition did explore and map a great deal of the West, and the naturalists who were on the trip contributed significantly to the scientific knowledge of that region.

Another Army topographical engineer who made very significant contributions to the exploration and mapping of the American West was John C. Fremont. Although he may not be as well known today as he was in the middle of the nineteenth century, he and his writings were incredibly influential in the overland settlement of the West. Many pioneers carried his books with them on their journeys, and Brigham Young was particularly influenced by Fremont's work when he established the Mormon settlement in the Salt Lake Valley.

Fremont, though not a West Point graduate, had the advantage of being the son-in-law of the very powerful Missouri senator Thomas Hart Benton, a great advocate of westward expansion. Fremont, as it turned out, had extensive cartographic expertise. In the late 1830s, as a protégé of Secretary of War Joel Poinsett (after whom the poinsettia is named), Fremont had been assigned to assist a French civilian engineer, Joseph Nicollet, in mapping the upper reaches of the Mississippi River basin. Fremont learned an enormous amount from Nicollet about geography, Native American cultures and scientific measurement (including the use of a barometer to measure the height of mountains).

Based on Fremont's expertise, Benton was able to convince Col. John J. Abert, commandant of the Corps of Topographical Engineers, to appoint Fremont to lead an expedition to the Rocky Mountains and, later, to Oregon and California. With him on those expeditions was a German topographer, Charles Preuss, who, in the 1840s and 1850s, drew some of the most iconic maps of the West.

On the first trek, in 1842, the party went up the Platte River and split up at the division of the North and South Platte. Those on the North Platte went up to Fort Laramie, in present-day Wyoming, and those on the South Platte went up to St. Vrain's Fort, in present-day Colorado. At the time, both were fur trading posts. The parties then met up at Fort Laramie, went up the Platte from there, to the Sweetwater River, through the South Pass of the Rocky Mountains, to the Wind River Mountains. There, Fremont climbed a mountain in the Wind River range since named for him. He used that image in his presidential campaign of 1856, as the first Republican nominee for president.

In his 1843–44 expedition Fremont returned to St. Vrain's Fort. He and his expedition then went through the Black Hills and proceeded along what was fast becoming an Emigrant Trail to Oregon. They then traveled to Fort Bridger (also in present-day Wyoming and also, at the time, a fur trading post). After leaving Fort Bridger, they crossed the Bear Mountains and followed the Bear River to the Great Salt Lake. After exploring the Great Salt Lake, they crossed over to the Snake River (formerly known as Lewis's Fork of the Columbia), and followed it, and Reid's River, to Fort

Boisée, in present-day Idaho. They followed the Snake and several of its tributaries, crossed the Blue Mountains to the Umatillah River, and continued on to the Valley of the Walla-Walla and to its intersection with the Columbia (where Fort Nez Percé, later known as Fort Walla Walla, was located). From there, Fremont went down the Valley of the Columbia to The Dalles, and from there, by canoe, to Fort Vancouver.

Fremont returned East by going through California. He went down what is now the Des Chutes River, to near its source; crossed over to several lakes in the area; went south, into what is now western Nevada, to the Mud Lakes and Pyramid Lake, and crossed the Salmon Trout River and Carson's and Walker's Rivers. Fremont then turned west and crossed the Sierra Nevada Mountains, ending up at Nueva Helvetia (Sutter's Fort) on the Sacramento River. He then went through the San Joaquin Valley; around the eastern shore of the Tulare Lakes; crossed the Sierra Nevadas at what is now Tehachapi Pass; struck the Old Spanish Trail from Los Angeles to Santa Fe; followed that Trail down the Mojave River and thence up to the Sevier River and Utah Lake, in what is now Utah. He then turned east, up the Spanish Fork; crossed the Wasatch Mountains and returned to the Green River and to St. Vrain's Fort.

In 1845 and 1846, Fremont again returned to the West. Exactly why he did so is not known. He may have been scouting a route for a Pacific Railroad, but, in any event, several members of his expedition died, he got involved in the Bear Flag Revolt in California, and he ended up being court-martialed for insubordination.

Fremont's accomplishments include: (1) his *Report* covering the 1842 and 1843–44 expeditions, which was used extensively by many emigrants to the West, and the accompanying illustrations that provided them with important visual context (e.g., Fort Laramie, an important stop on what became the Oregon Trail [fig. 21]); (2) a map of the 1843–44 route that, on its face, first describes the Great Basin: "diameter 11° of latitude, 10° of longitude; elevation above the sea between 4 and 5000 feet; surrounded by lofty mountains; contents almost unknown, but believed to be filled with rivers and lakes which have no communication with the sea" (fig. 22) (though both Benjamin Bonneville and Joseph Walker would later be credited with that discovery); and (3) a description of the Salt Lake Valley that encouraged Brigham Young and many Mormons to settle there.

THE US ARMY IN THE MEXICAN WAR

The southwestern part of the United States was not well explored or mapped by 1845 and the first real reconnaissance of that area was conducted by a detachment of Fremont's third expedition, headed by Lt. James Abert (the son of the head of the Corps of Topographical Engineers) and Lt. William Peck. Their task was to explore and map the southern Rockies, in the possible event of military operations in that area. Their report and map provided very useful information about New Mexico.

After the Mexican War began in 1846, the exploration and mapping of the Southwest accelerated. The leader in this effort was a West Point graduate and topographical engineer named William H. Emory, whose contributions to western mapping have been said to rival those of Lewis and

Clark and Fremont. Emory, who was raised on a plantation on the Eastern Shore of Maryland, was descended from distinguished Americans: his grandfather had fought in the Revolutionary War, and his father in the War of 1812. He was offered an appointment to West Point by John C. Calhoun when he was only eleven years old. Emory, like Fremont, had served as an assistant to Joseph Nicollet during the exploration of the upper Mississippi River basin. Emory had also served on an expedition to map the northeast boundary of the United States, and he had headed a party to map west Texas, as far as the Rio Grande, in 1844.

In 1846, President James K. Polk directed Gen. Stephen Watts Kearny to proceed west from Fort Leavenworth in what is now Kansas, with his "Army of the West," capture New Mexico, and proceed to San Diego and Los Angeles to take California from Mexico. Emory was assigned to Kearny as his topographical engineer. Following this expedition, Emory produced a narrative of the trip and a comprehensive map (fig. 23), both of which were utilized by travelers for many years.

Kearny basically took the Santa Fe Trail to Bent's Fort (in present-day Colorado, and the only American outpost on the Santa Fe Trail for many years), and then crossed the Raton Pass into New Mexico and captured Las Vegas, New Mexico and Santa Fe. With New Mexico secure, Kearny then set out for San Diego, California with 300 troops and 14 topographical personnel. Kearny directed Capt. Philip St. George Cooke to lead a Mormon battalion that had been "recruited" and go south of the mountains and the Gila River that were west of Santa Fe and Albuquerque, to establish a wagon road to California (fig. 24). In the meantime, two other topographical engineers, Lieutenant Abert and Lieutenant Peck (who had earlier been with Fremont) were detailed to perform a reconnaissance of the newly conquered territory of New Mexico (fig. 25). In addition to useful geographical and topographical information, the reports of these explorations included descriptions and illustrations of the flora and fauna along the routes (fig. 26).

Not far west of Albuquerque, Kearny and his train were approached from the west by legendary frontiersman Kit Carson, who advised them California had surrendered. Therefore, Kearny sent 200 of his men back to Santa Fe and continued west with only 100 men (including Emory). Not far from San Diego, Kearny's force was attacked by Mexicans who were trying to re-take Southern California. Kearny's troops and others subsequently re-captured Los Angeles, and the war for California was essentially over. The Treaty of Guadalupe-Hidalgo of 1848 ended the Mexican War, and the United States received what is now California, Arizona north of the Gila River, most of Utah and Nevada and parts of New Mexico, Colorado and Wyoming.

20

STEPHEN HARRIMAN LONG (1784–1864)

[Detail from:] *MAP OF ARKANSAS AND OTHER TERRITORIES OF THE UNITED STATES RESPECTFULLY INSCRIBED TO THE HON. J. CALHOUN, SECRETARY OF WAR*

Engraved By Young & Delleker. 14⅝ x 14⅜. From: *A Complete Historical, Chronological, and Geographical American Atlas* (Philadelphia: Carey & Lea, 1822).

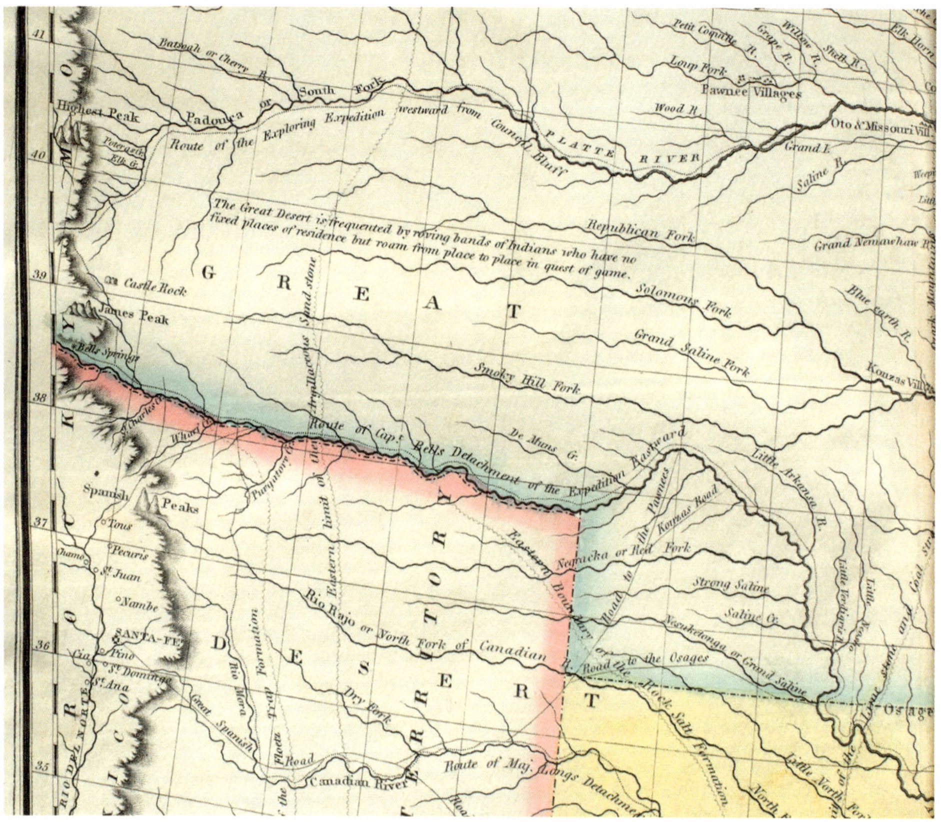

This map detail shows the "Highest Peak" (later named Pike's Peak), located at the upper left, and below it, James Peak (named after the botanist on the expedition, Dr. Edwin James), and places the name "Great Desert" on a portion of the West that settlers would avoid for decades.

21

FORT LARAMIE

Baltimore: E. Weber & Co. Lithograph, 7 x 4¼ in. From: John C. Fremont: *Report of the Exploring Expedition to the Rocky Mountains in the Year 1842, and to Oregon and North California in the Years 1843-'44.* 28th Cong., 2nd Sess., Senate Ex. Doc. No. 174, Serial 461 (Washington: Gales and Seaton, 1845).

Other than the announcements that gold had been discovered in California, perhaps nothing encouraged western migration more than John C. Fremont's *Report of the Exploring Expedition to the Rocky Mountains in the Year 1842 and to Oregon and North California in the Years 1843-'44.* Prior to Fremont, earlier explorers like Pike and Long had described much of the Southwest as a desert. Fremont's expedition provided much detail about the soil, water, geology, flora and fauna, and made the argument that much of this land was arable. Many, such as Brigham Young, were encouraged by these data.

FORT LARAMIE

22

JOHN C. FREMONT (1813–1890) AND CHARLES PREUSS (1803–1854)
MAP OF AN EXPLORING EXPEDITION TO THE ROCKY MOUNTAINS IN THE YEAR 1842, OREGON & NORTH CALIFORNIA IN THE YEARS 1843–44

Baltimore: E. Weber & Co., 1845. 51⅛ x 30½ in. From: *Report of the Exploring Expedition to the Rocky Mountains in the Year 1842, and to Oregon and North California in the Years 1843–'44*, 28th Cong., 2nd Sess., Senate Ex. Doc. No. 174, Serial 461 (1845).

On its face, this map appears to be a preliminary or partial draft, with large areas of blank space. However, that is because Fremont portrayed only the area he and his party had actually explored and measured. During his journey, Fremont circled the Great Basin and publicized its true interior drainage, which is portrayed on the map, though he erroneously assumed large mountain ranges ran east and west to the north and south of the Great Basin.

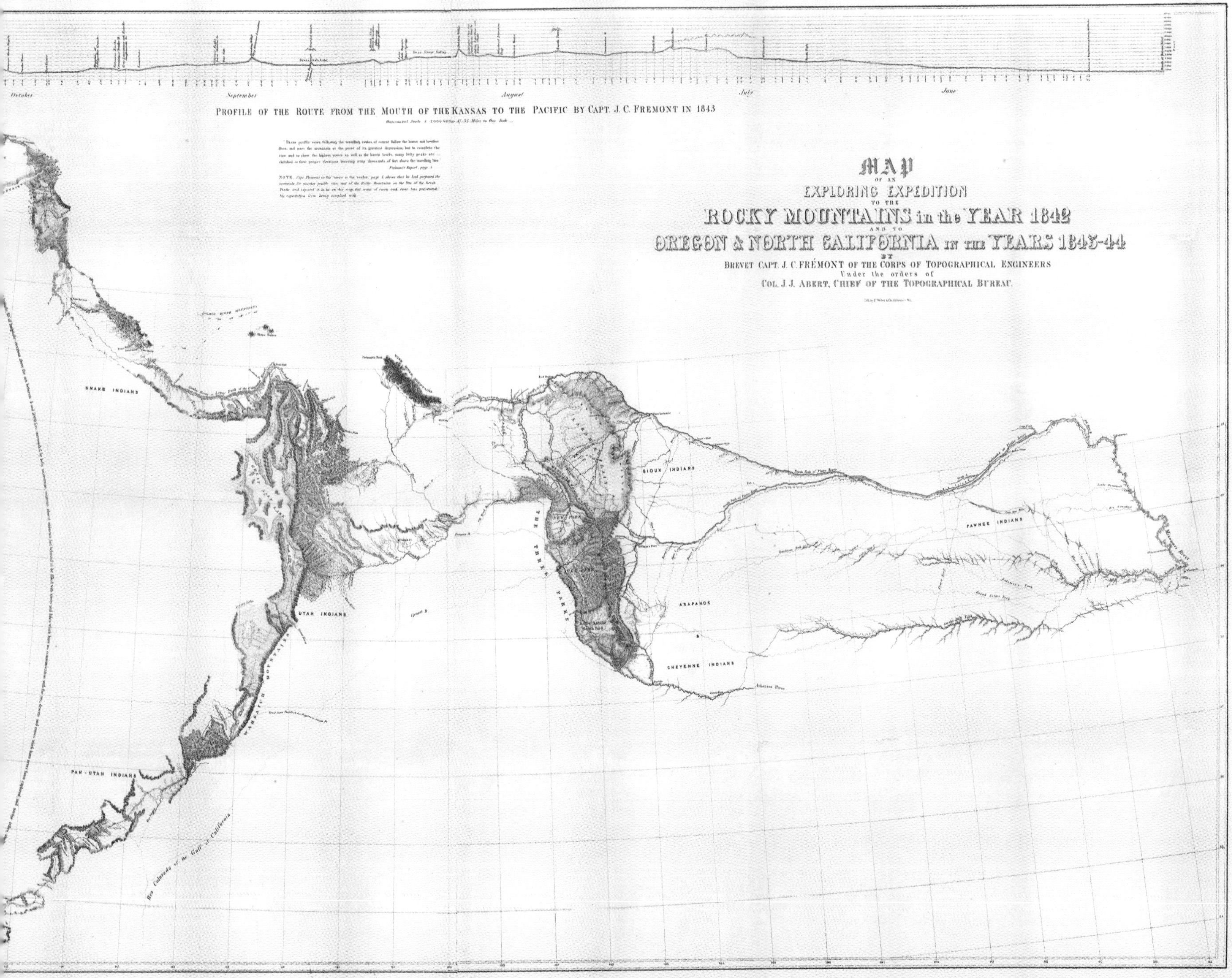

October
September
August
July
June
PROFILE OF THE ROUTE FROM THE MOUTH OF THE KANSAS TO THE PACIFIC BY CAPT. J. C. FREMONT IN 1843
MAP
OF AN
EXPLORING EXPEDITION
TO THE
ROCKY MOUNTAINS in the YEAR 1842
AND TO
OREGON & NORTH CALIFORNIA IN THE YEARS 1843-44
BY
BREVET CAPT. J. C. FRÉMONT OF THE CORPS OF TOPOGRAPHICAL ENGINEERS
Under the orders of
COL. J. J. ABERT, CHIEF OF THE TOPOGRAPHICAL BUREAU.
SNAKE INDIANS
SIOUX INDIANS
PAWNEE INDIANS
UTAH INDIANS
ARAPAHOE
CHEYENNE INDIANS
PAH-UTAH INDIANS
THE THREE PARKS

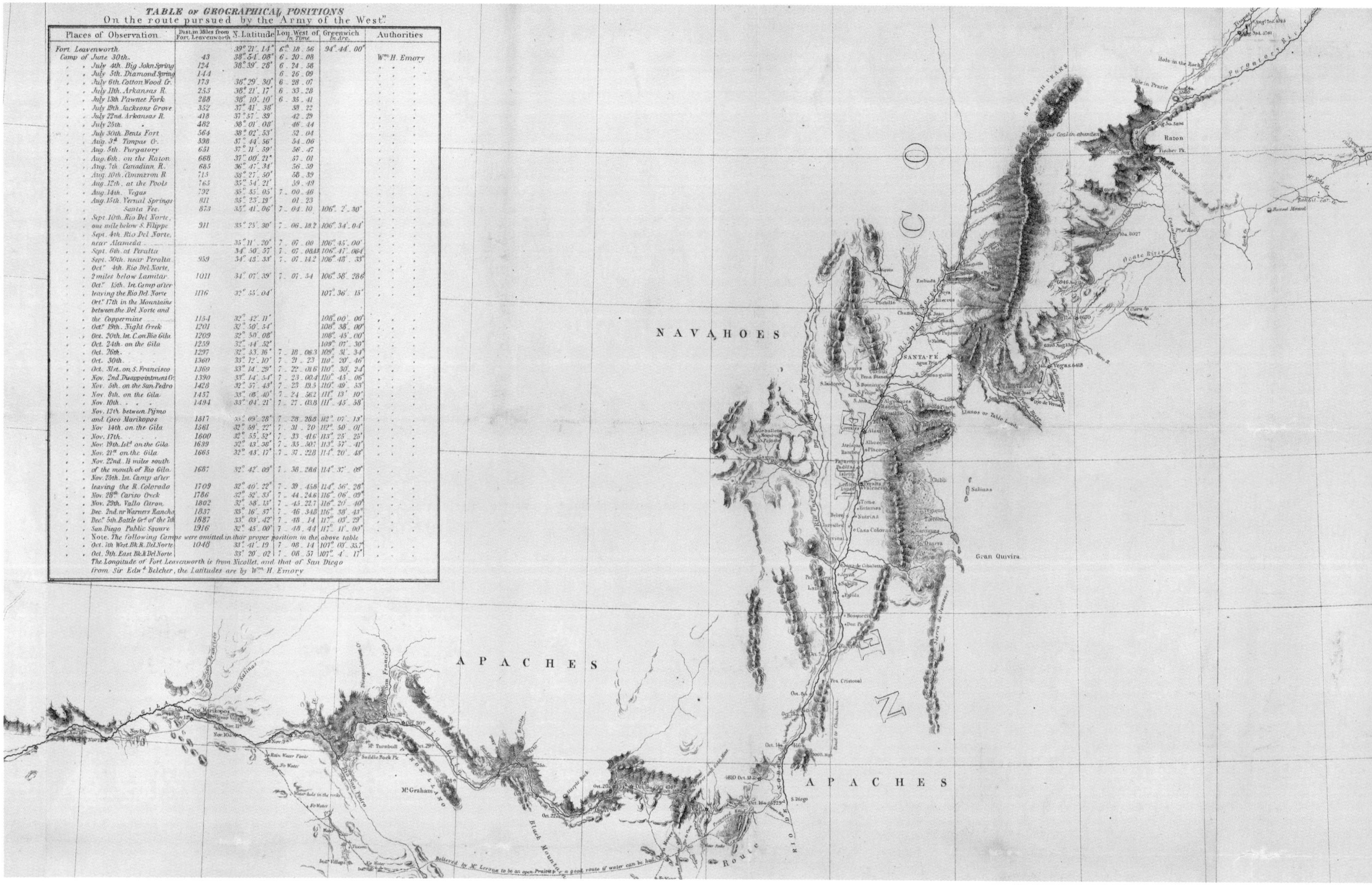

TABLE OF GEOGRAPHICAL POSITIONS
On the route pursued by the "Army of the West."

Places of Observation	Dist. in Miles from Fort Leavenworth	N. Latitude	Lon. West of Greenwich In Time	In Arc	Authorities
Fort Leavenworth		39° 21' 14"	6h 18 56	94° 44' 00"	
Camp of June 30th.	43	38° 54' 08"	6 20 08		Wm. H. Emory
July 4th. Big John Spring	124	38° 39' 28"	6 24 58		. . .
July 5th. Diamond Spring	144		6 26 09		. . .
July 6th. Cotton Wood Cr.	173	38° 29' 30"	6 28 07		. . .
July 11th. Arkansas R.	253	38° 21' 17"	6 33 28		. . .
July 13th Pawnee Fork	288	38° 10' 10"	6 35 41		. . .
July 19th Jacksons Grove	352	37° 41' 38"	38 22		. . .
July 22nd. Arkansas R.	418	37° 57' 39"	42 29		. . .
July 25th.	482	38° 01' 08"	46 44		. . .
July 30th. Bents Fort	564	38° 02' 53"	52 04		. . .
Aug. 3d Timpas Cr.	598	37° 44' 56"	54 06		. . .
Aug. 5th. Purgatory	651	37° 11' 59"	56 47		. . .
Aug. 6th. on the Raton	668	37° 00' 21"	57 01		. . .
Aug. 7th. Canadian R.	685	36° 47' 34"	56 59		. . .
Aug. 10th. Cimmeron R	715	36° 27' 50"	58 39		. . .
Aug. 12th. at the Pools	765	35° 54' 21"	59 49		. . .
Aug. 14th. Vegas	792	35° 35' 05"	7 00 46		. . .
Aug. 15th. Vernal Springs	811	35° 23' 19"	01 23		. . .
Santa Fee.	873	35° 41' 06"	7 04 10	106° 2' 30"	. . .
Sept. 10th. Rio Del Norte, one mile below S. Filippe	911	35° 25' 30"	7 06 18.2	106° 34' 04"	. . .
Sept. 4th. Rio Del Norte, near Alameda		35° 11' 20"	7 07 00	106° 45' 00"	. . .
Sept. 6th. at Peralta		34° 50' 57"	7 07 0843	106° 47' 064	. . .
Sept. 30th. near Peralta	959	34° 43' 33"	7 07 14.2	106° 48' 33"	. . .
Octr 4th. Rio Del Norte, 2 miles below Lamitar	1011	34° 07' 39"	7 07 54	106° 58' 286	. . .
Octr 15th. 1st. Camp after leaving the Rio Del Norte	1116	32° 55' 04"		107° 36' 15"	. . .
Octr 17th in the Mountains between the Del Norte and the Coppermine	1154	32° 42' 11"		108° 00' 00"	. . .
Octr 19th. Night Creek	1201	32° 50' 54"		108° 38' 00"	. . .
Oct. 20th. 1st. C. on Rio Gila	1209	32° 50' 08"		108° 45' 00"	. . .
Oct. 24th. on the Gila	1259	32° 44' 52"		109° 07' 30"	. . .
Oct. 26th.	1297	32° 53' 16"	7 18 06.3	109° 31' 34"	. . .
Oct. 30th.	1360	33° 12' 10"	7 21 23	110° 20' 46"	. . .
Oct. 31st. on S. Francisco	1369	33° 14' 29"	7 22 01.6	110° 30' 24"	. . .
Nov. 2nd. Disappointment Cr.	1390	33° 14' 54"	7 23 00.4	110° 45' 06"	. . .
Nov. 5th. on the San Pedro	1428	32° 57' 43"	7 23 19.5	110° 49' 53"	. . .
Nov. 8th. on the Gila	1457	33° 05' 40"	7 24 56.2	111° 13' 10"	. . .
Nov. 10th.	1494	33° 04' 21"	7 27 03.8	111° 45' 58"	. . .
Nov. 12th between Pijmo and Coco Marikopos	1517	33° 09' 28"	7 28 28.8	112° 07' 13"	. . .
Nov 14th. on the Gila	1561	32° 59' 22"	7 31 20	112° 50' 01"	. . .
Nov. 17th.	1600	32° 55' 52"	7 33 41.6	113° 25' 25"	. . .
Nov. 19th. Isld on the Gila	1639	32° 43' 38"	7 35 50.7	113° 57' 41"	. . .
Nov. 21st on the Gila	1665	32° 43' 17"	7 37 22.8	114° 20' 43"	. . .
Nov. 22nd. 1½ miles south of the mouth of Rio Gila	1687	32° 42' 09"	7 38 28.6	114° 37' 09"	. . .
Nov. 25th. 1st. Camp after leaving the R. Colorado	1709	32° 40' 22"	7 39 45.8	114° 56' 28"	. . .
Nov. 28th Cariso Creek	1786	32° 52' 33"	7 44 24.6	116° 06' 09"	. . .
Nov. 29th. Vallo Citron	1802	32° 58' 15"	7 45 22.7	116° 20' 40"	. . .
Dec. 2nd. nr Warners Rancho	1837	33° 16' 57"	7 46 34.8	116° 38' 43"	. . .
Decr 5th. Battle Grd of the 7th	1887	33° 03' 42"	7 48 14	117° 03' 29"	. . .
San Diego Public Square	1916	32° 45' 00"	7 48 44	117° 11' 00"	. . .
Note. The following Camps were omitted in their proper position in the above table					
Oct. 7th West Bk. R. Del Norte	1048	33° 41' 19	7 08 14	107° 03' 35.7"	. . .
Oct. 9th. East Bk. R. Del Norte		33° 20' 02	7 08 57	107° 4' 17"	. . .

The Longitude of Fort Leavenworth is from Nicollet, and that of San Diego from Sir Edwd. Belcher, the Latitudes are by Wm. H. Emory

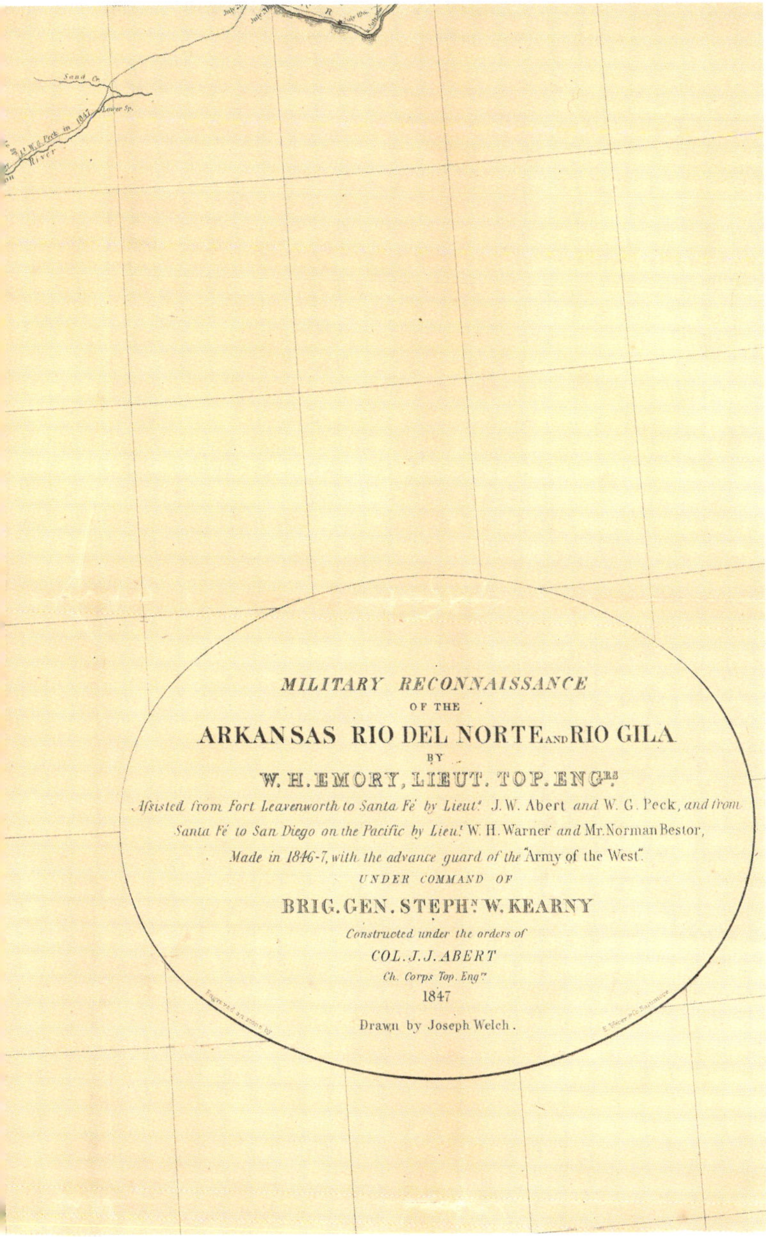

23

W. H. EMORY (1811–1887) · [Detail from:]

MILITARY RECONNAISSANCE OF THE ARKANSAS, RIO DEL NORTE AND RIO GILA BY W. H. EMORY, LIEUT. TOP. ENGRS. ASSISTED FROM FORT LEAVENWORTH TO SANTA FÉ BY LIEUTS. J. W. ABERT AND W. G. PECK, AND FROM SANTA FÉ TO SAN DIEGO ON THE PACIFIC BY LIEUT. W. H. WARNER AND MR. NORMAN BESTOR, MADE IN 1846–7, WITH THE ADVANCE GUARD OF THE "ARMY OF THE WEST," UNDER COMMAND OF BRIG. GEN. STEPH^{N} KEARNY

Drawn By Joseph Welch. Baltimore: E. Weber & Co., 1847. 64¾ x 30 in.
From: *Notes of a Military Reconnoissance, from Fort Leavenworth in Missouri, to San Diego, in California, including Part of the Arkansas, Del Norte and Gila Rivers. By Lieut. Col. W. H. Emory Made in 1846–7, with the Advanced Guard of the "Army of the West,"* 30th Cong., 1st Sess., House Doc. 41, Serial 517 (Washington, DC: Wendell and Van Benthuysen, 1848).

Emory was Gen. Stephen Watts Kearny's chief topographical engineer, and this map is generally known as "Emory's Map." Prepared by topographical engineers, it provided much-needed detail for military maneuvers and subsequent exploration of what became the American Southwest.

24

W. H. EMORY (1811–1887) · [Detail from:] *SKETCH OF PART OF THE MARCH & WAGON ROAD OF LT. COL. COOKE, FROM SANTA FE TO THE PACIFIC OCEAN, 1846–7*

Philadelphia: P. S. Duval, 1848. 15½ x 22½ in. From: *Notes of a Military Reconnoissance, from Fort Leavenworth in Missouri, to San Diego, in California, including Part of the Arkansas, Del Norte and Gila Rivers. By Lieut. Col. W. H. Emory Made in 1846–7, with the Advanced Guard of the "Army of the West,"* 30th Cong., 1st Sess., House Doc. 41, Serial 517 (Washington: Wendell and Van Benthuysen, 1848).

Cooke's Wagon Road map was important because it illustrated that the route he took (which was essentially along the 32nd parallel of north latitude) was an excellent one for a possible railroad; the Southern Pacific Railroad was later to run along this route. However, the problem was that, even after the 1848 Treaty of Guadalupe-Hidalgo (which ended the Mexican War, and gave what became the American Southwest to the US), the US didn't own most of the land over which Cooke's Wagon Road ran. Therefore, in 1853, James Gadsden, the United States minister to Mexico, acquired a tract of land from Mexico that has been referred to ever since as the Gadsden Purchase, to insure that a railroad could be built across that stretch of country.

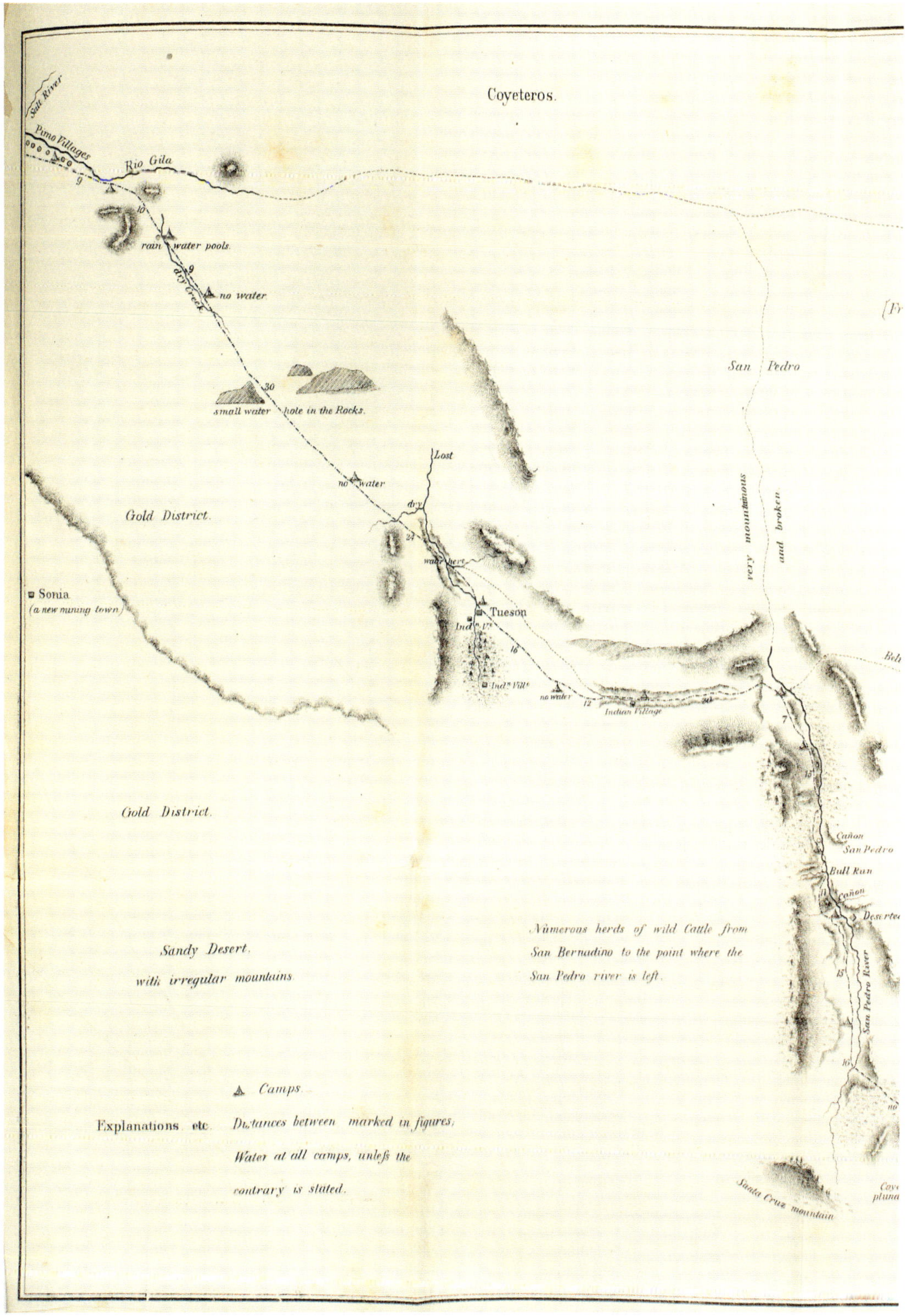

Coyeteros.
Salt River
Pimo Villages
Rio Gila
rain water pools.
dry creek
no water.
small water hole in the Rocks.
Lost
no water
dry
water here
Gold District.
Sonia
(a new mining town)
Tucson
Ind. Vill.
no water
Indian Village
San Pedro
very mountainous and broken
Cañon San Pedro
Bull Run
Cañon
Gold District.
Numerous herds of wild Cattle from San Bernadino to the point where the San Pedro river is left.
San Pedro River
Sandy Desert.
with irregular mountains.
Camps.
Explanations etc.
Distances between marked in figures.
Water at all camps, unless the contrary is stated.
Santa Cruz mountain

62]

UTAH INDIANS
High broken Table Lands
DATA.
Topographical sketches by Lieut W.G. Peck, T.E.
This map is connected with the map of Senate Document, N°438, 2nd Session, 29th Congress.
PUBLISHED BY ORDER OF THE WAR DEPARTMENT
NAVAJO INDIANS
SANTA FE
High Table Lands, no running water
APACHE
INDIANS
RIO DEL NORTE
MAP
of the
TERRITORY OF NEW MEXICO,
made by order of
BRIG. GEN. S.W. KEARNY,
under instructions from
LIEUT. W. H. EMORY, U.S.T.E.
by
1846-7.
Scale of Miles

25

JAMES W. ABERT (1820–1897) AND WILLIAM G. PECK (1820–1892)

MAP OF THE TERRITORY OF NEW MEXICO, MADE BY ORDER OF BRIG. GEN. S. W. KEARNY, UNDER INSTRUCTIONS FROM LIEUT. W. H. EMORY, U.S.T.E. BY LIEUTS. J. W. ABERT AND W. G. PECK, U.S.T.E. 1846–7. TOPOGRAPHICAL SKETCHES BY LT. W. G. PECK, T.E.

Washington: War Department and C. B. Graham's Lith., 1848. 24⅜ x 19⅛ in. From: *Notes of a Military Reconnoissance, from Fort Leavenworth in Missouri, to San Diego, in California, including Part of the Arkansas, Del Norte and Gila Rivers. By Lieut. Col. W. H. Emory Made in 1846–7, with the Advanced Guard of the "Army of the West,"* 30th Cong., 1st Sess., House Doc. 41, Serial 517 (Washington: Wendell and Van Benthuysen, 1848).

While General Kearny and Lieutenant Colonel Emory were on the way to California, two topographical engineers were detailed to explore and map what became New Mexico at the conclusion of the Mexican War.

26

JOHN MIX STANLEY (1814-1872)
CEREUS GIGANTEUS

Washington: C. B. Graham. 1848. Lithograph, 4 x 6¾ in. From: *Notes of a Military Reconnoissance, from Fort Leavenworth in Missouri, to San Diego, in California, including Part of the Arkansas, Del Norte and Gila Rivers. By Lieut. Col. W. H. Emory Made in 1846-7, with the Advanced Guard of the "Army of the West,"* 30th Cong., 1st Sess., House Doc. 41, Serial 517 (Washington, DC: Wendell and Van Benthuysen, 1848).

Early in the Mexican War, the United States military command realized that accurate data regarding northern Mexico were not available to US troops. Therefore, Army expeditions were often accompanied by topographical engineers and other scientists whose job was to gather information that could be used by the army. Emory's report was a comprehensive summary of Gen. Stephen Watts Kearny's journey, measurements made along the way, and information regarding the flora and fauna observed during the expedition. John Mix Stanley was an accomplished artist and later became extremely well-known for his western American art.

IV

MARKETING THE WEST

A. SANTA FE AND TEXAS: TRADING ALONG THE SANTA FE TRAIL AND SETTLING TEXAS

THE SANTA FE TRAIL

AMERICAN TRADERS sought to go to Santa Fe, a town that had been established by the Spanish in 1610, from shortly after the Louisiana Purchase was completed. However, as the experience of Zebulon Montgomery Pike illustrated, the Spanish were not hospitable toward Americans. All that changed in 1821, when Mexico threw off the Spanish yoke. The Mexican government realized that it needed trading partners, and trade between the United States and Santa Fe became a reality in that year. The original Santa Fe Trail ran from near Independence, Missouri, through Westport, in what is now Kansas City, across present-day Kansas, to the Arkansas River, up that river to Bent's Fort, in what is now Colorado, and through the Raton Pass, into New Mexico, and to Santa Fe. (Bent's Fort was not a military installation, but a fur-trading center, founded by Bent, St. Vrain & Co. in the early 1830s. Despite the absence of military personnel, Bent's Fort was a very common stopping place for travelers.)

It soon became apparent that the route to Santa Fe through the mountains was not conducive to wagon travel. Therefore, in 1822, William Becknell sought to locate a wagon road to Santa Fe. He headed south of the Arkansas River before it reached the mountains, and came upon the Cimarron River. The source of the Cimarron was near Santa Fe and thereafter, the so-called Cimarron Cutoff became an alternate route of the Santa Fe Trail.

It wasn't long before traders and others began to write narratives and provide maps for potential traders and settlers. Josiah Gregg, one of the earliest recorded travelers who went to the Southwest for his health, became a Santa Fe trader in the early 1830s. In 1844, he published a book on his activities on the Santa Fe Trail, which was enormously popular and went through several editions (fig. 27). The map in his book was extremely accurate, and an excellent portrayal of the Santa Fe Trail (fig. 28). As the tide of emigrants began to swell, particularly after the discovery of gold in California was widely publicized, new routes west were explored, and maps were created specifically for use by emigrants to Santa Fe and beyond (fig. 29).

TEXAS

The American Southwest had been settled by the Spanish beginning in the middle of the sixteenth century. However, the Spanish never really found great wealth there, as they had in Mexico and parts of South America, so the few settlers there were mostly involved in agriculture and saving souls. In 1762, France ceded to Spain the territory that was later to be included in the Louisiana Purchase, and the Spanish then found themselves far closer to British North America than they wanted. This led them to map and set up defensive positions in the northern parts of their North American possessions. In the early 1820s, in an effort to populate the northern parts of this new territory, the Spanish began to issue land grants to potential settlers in what is now Texas, and encouraged the settlers to recruit other families to move to the area. One of the first grantees was a Connecticut-born entrepreneur named Moses Austin, who developed and managed lead mines in Virginia and in the area around Ste. Genevieve, Missouri. After the Panic of 1819, Austin went to San Antonio and obtained a land grant, but died before he could settle it. That task fell to his son, Stephen F. Austin. The younger Austin had to renegotiate his father's land grant with the Mexican government, since Mexico had declared its independence from Spain in 1821. Though Mexico had initially encouraged Americans to settle in Texas, Anglo settlers in the area soon became so numerous that Mexico cut off American colonization in 1830. Relations subsequently deteriorated between Mexico and the settlers, and in 1835, Texas declared itself independent of Mexico (fig. 30). After the Alamo, the Goliad massacre and the Battle of San Jacinto, the Mexicans withdrew, but they did not recognize the Republic of Texas. Texas was annexed to the United States in 1845, and that activity served as one of the triggers for the Mexican War.

27

JOSIAH GREGG (1806–1850)

COMMERCE OF THE PRAIRIES: OR THE JOURNAL OF A SANTA FÉ TRADER, DURING EIGHT EXPEDITIONS ACROSS THE GREAT WESTERN PRAIRIES, AND A RESIDENCE OF NEARLY NINE YEARS IN NORTHERN MEXICO

New York: Henry G. Langley, 1844.

Gregg's book was filled with information about western geography, flora and fauna, and Native American and Spanish cultures in the Southwest. His map of the Santa Fe Trail was very accurate. Born in Tennessee, Gregg moved to Missouri, studied law, developed pulmonary problems and was told by his doctor to move to the Southwest. After working for a Santa Fe trader, he became one himself and later brought the first printing press to Santa Fe.

28

JOSIAH GREGG (1806–1850)

A MAP OF THE INDIAN TERRITORY, NORTHERN TEXAS AND NEW MEXICO SHOWING THE GREAT WESTERN PRAIRIES

New York: Morse & Breese, 1844. 12½ x 15 in. From: *Commerce of the Prairies: or The Journal of a Santa Fé Trader, During Eight Expeditions Across the Great Western Prairies, and a Residence of Nearly Nine Years in Northern Mexico* (New York: Henry G. Langley, 1844).

This map shows the route of the Santa Fe Trail and other routes taken by explorers and emigrants.

A MAP OF THE
INDIAN TERRITORY
NORTHERN TEXAS
AND
NEW MEXICO
Showing the
GREAT WESTERN PRAIRIES
by
JOSIAH GREGG
EXPLANATION
HUNTING GROUNDS OF THE
PAWNEES, KANZAS, OTOES,
AND OTHERS
LLANO ESTACADO
or
STAKED PLAINS
INDIAN TERRITORY
MEXICO

29

JAMES H. SIMPSON (1813-1883) · *MAP NO. 4, SHOWING CONTINUATION OF FORT SMITH AND SANTA FE ROUTE, FROM TUCUMCARI CREEK TO SANTA FE . . . 1849*

Philadelphia: P. S. Duval's Lith. Steam Press, 1850. 18⅝ x 12½ in. From: *Report from the Secretary of War, Communicating, in Compliance with a Resolution of the Senate, the Report and Map of the Route from Fort Smith, Arkansas, to Santa Fe, New Mexico*, 31st Cong., 1st Sess., Senate Doc. No. 12, Serial 554 (Washington, 1850).

This map is the fourth in the set that begins with the *Map of the Route Pursued by U. S. Troops from Fort Smith, Arkansas, to Santa Fe, New Mexico, via South Side of Canadian River in the Year 1849, whilst Serving as an Escort to a Party of California Emigrants*. Drawn by topographical engineer Lt. James H. Simpson, it was designed to be used by tradesmen, settlers and fortune hunters to guide them across the terrain to reach Santa Fe, much as American Automobile Association maps would be used, a century later, to provide travelers guidance on America's roads. Note that one source of water is said to have "fish with legs."

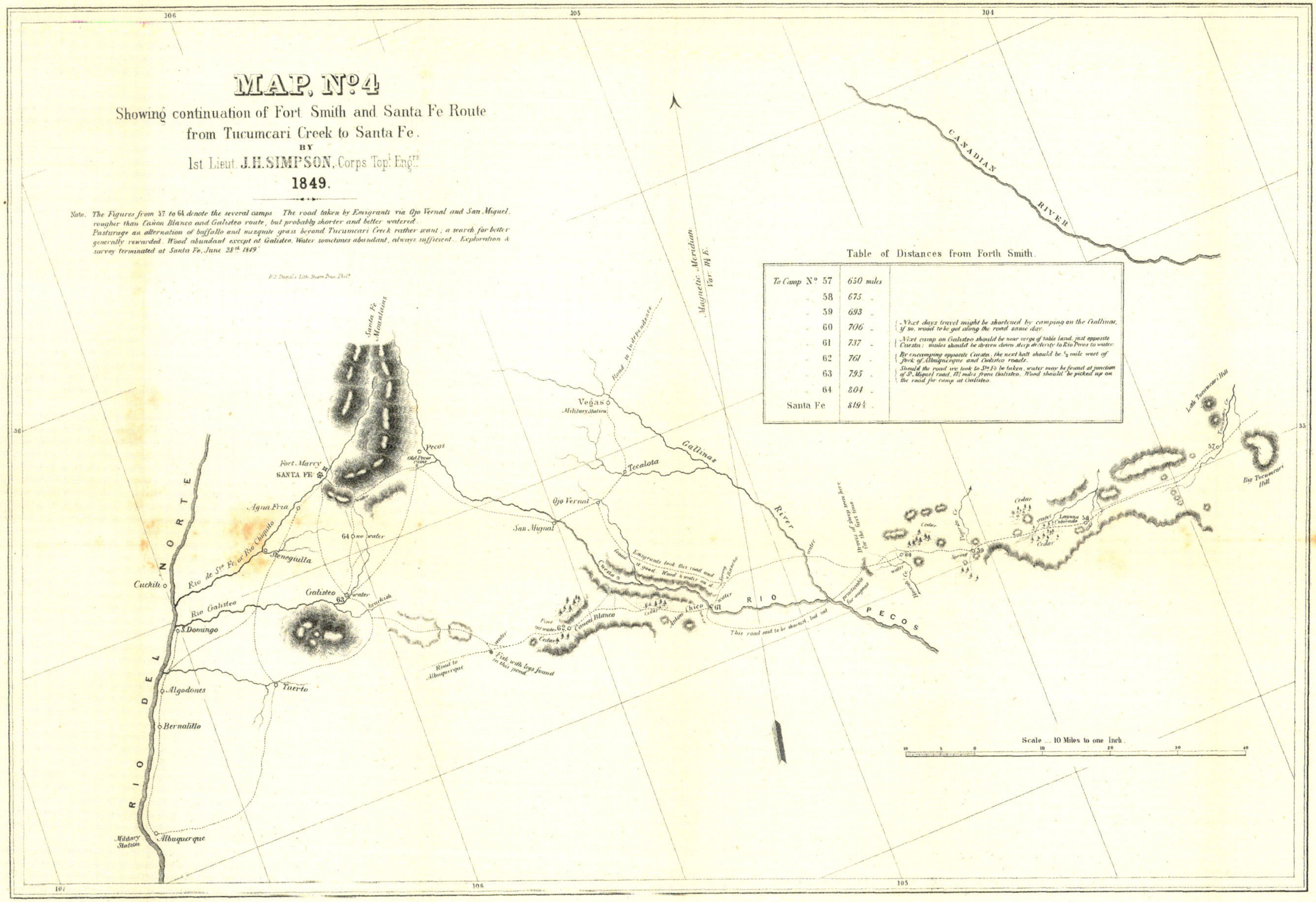
MAP, No. 4
Showing continuation of Fort Smith and Santa Fe Route
from Tucumcari Creek to Santa Fe.
BY
1st Lieut. J.H.SIMPSON, Corps Topl. Engrs.
1849.
Note. The Figures from 57 to 64 denote the several camps. The road taken by Emigrants via Ojo Vernal and San Miguel, rougher than Cañon Blanco and Galisteo route, but probably shorter and better watered.
Pasturage an alternation of buffalo and mezquite grass beyond Tucumcari Creek rather scant; a search for better generally rewarded. Wood abundant except at Galisteo. Water sometimes abundant, always sufficient. Exploration & survey terminated at Santa Fe, June 28th 1849.
Table of Distances from Forth Smith.
To Camp No. 57 650 miles
58 675
59 693
60 706 Next days travel might be shortened by camping on the Gallinas, if so, wood to be got along the road same day.
61 737 Next camp on Galisteo should be near verge of table land, just opposite Cuesta: mules should be driven down steep declivity to Rio Pecos to water.
62 761 By encamping opposite Cuesta, the next halt should be ½ mile west of fork of Albuquerque and Galisteo roads.
63 795 Should the road we took to Sta. Fe be taken, water may be found at junction of St. Miguel road, 13½ miles from Galisteo. Wood should be picked up on the road for camp at Galisteo.
64 804
Santa Fe 819½
CANADIAN RIVER
Santa Fe Mountains
Magnetic Meridian Var. 14° E.
Road to Independence
Vegas
Military Station
Gallinas River
Tecalota
Pecos
Fort Marcy
SANTA FE
Agua Fria
Ojo Vernal
San Miguel
Rio de Sta. Fe or Rio Chiquito
Cienequilla
Galisteo
Rio Galisteo
S. Domingo
Cuchilo
RIO DEL NORTE
Algodones
Tuerto
Bernalillo
Military Station
Albuquerque
Road to Albuquerque
Cañon Blanco
Cuesta
Anton Chico
RIO PECOS
Cedar
Laguna Colorado
Little Tucumcari Hill
Big Tucumcari Hill
Scale ... 10 Miles to one Inch

30

T. G. BRADFORD (1802–1887) · *TEXAS*

Boston: T. G. Bradford, 1838. 14 x 11½ in. From: *An Illustrated Atlas, Geographical, Statistical, and Historical, of the United States and the Adjacent Countries* (Boston: Weeks, Jordan, 1838).

This map, commercially produced in the late 1830s, after Texas declared its independence from Mexico, shows many of the land grants in what ultimately became southern and eastern Texas.

B. OREGON: PURSUING THE FUR TRADE, CONVERTING THE NATIVE AMERICANS, AND FARMING THE LAND

THE FUR TRAPPERS AND TRADERS

At the time of the Lewis and Clark expedition, not much was known about the Pacific Northwest. However, two things were known, from French and British traders: the area was full of fur-bearing animals, and there was money in furs. So, even on their way back east from the Pacific, Lewis and Clark crossed paths with fur trappers heading west. In fact, one member of the Lewis and Clark expedition, John Coulter, asked permission to join a group of trappers heading west. (During his travels, Coulter would explore an area referred to as "Coulter's Hell," now known as the volcanically active part of Yellowstone National Park.)

In 1810, John Jacob Astor, a German who lived in London and then New York, and who had made a fortune in the fur trade (and later in real estate), decided to open a fur trading post at the mouth of the Columbia River, which traverses through the Pacific Northwest. An overland party that essentially followed the Lewis and Clark route established Astoria in April 1811, the first American community on the west coast. Even though no significant discoveries were made by the westbound Astorians, a group of them, returning east in 1812, discovered what was subsequently named "South Pass," the most negotiable route over the Rocky Mountains, and the one that would be used by the majority of western emigrants to both Oregon and California prior to the advent of the railroads. Numerous authors, including Astorians Alexander Ross and Ross Cox, wrote about Astoria. However, by far the best-known and popular account was by Washington Irving, who Astor commissioned to write the official history of the expedition. The book contained a map that showed both the westbound and eastbound routes of the Astorians (fig. 31).

In 1837, Washington Irving produced another book covering a similar subject, this time based on the manuscript account of Capt. Benjamin Bonneville's multi-year journey through the inter-mountain West. Bonneville, a French-born West Point graduate, was serving in the army in the early 1830s, when he became fascinated with the idea of western exploration. He was granted a leave of absence from the army to explore the West and provide such intelligence as he could gather back to the government. The leave of absence lasted five years. In 1832, financed by John Jacob Astor and the American Fur Company, Bonneville led 110 men up the Platte River, through the South Pass and to the Green River, in present-day Wyoming, where they set up a trading post that they named Fort Bonneville.

In 1833, Bonneville and part of the group went up the Snake River (originally named Lewis's River, for Meriwether Lewis) into Idaho, and traded with the Shoshone Indians. Bonneville's explorations continued, finally reaching Fort Nez Percé in 1834, an outpost of the British Hudson's Bay Company, in present-day Washington State. After his return east, Bonneville rejoined the army (he had been stricken from the rolls, due to his lengthy absence), fought in the Mexican War and the Civil War, and died in 1878.

Irving's book contains two maps that Bonneville created during his explorations. The first shows much of the territory west of the Rocky Mountains (fig. 32), and the other shows the sources of a large number of western rivers and the Great Salt Lake (fig. 33).

THE MISSIONARIES

Spanish friars began to establish missions to convert Native Americans to Christianity as early as the 1530s. Beginning in 1769, Father Junipero Serra and a group of Franciscans established a number of missions in Alta California, including in San Diego, San Fernando, Santa Barbara and San Francisco. In the early nineteenth century, missionaries from various denominations in the United States began to move to the far West, including Congregationalist minister Samuel Parker, and Dr. Marcus Whitman, a Presbyterian. In 1835, Parker and Whitman preached to the fur trappers and traders at their annual rendezvous, on the Green River in what is now Wyoming. While Whitman returned East, Parker kept going west, visiting Fort Vancouver on the Columbia River, a British Hudson's Bay Trading Company outpost. He then scouted the Willamette Valley and the Columbia River Valley for mission sites. After Parker returned East, he recounted his experiences in a book entitled *Journal of an Exploring Tour Beyond the Rocky Mountains, Under the Direction of the A.B.C.F.M.* [*American Board of Commissioners for Foreign Missions*] *Performed in the Years 1835, '36 and '37* (Ithaca, NY, 1838). Parker's book also included his up-to-date map of the Oregon Territory. Both the book and the excellent map were widely used by emigrants to Oregon (fig. 34).

Another early missionary was Father Pierre-Jean De Smet, a Belgian Jesuit priest who began his missionary work among the Native Americans of the Pacific Northwest in 1840. Father De Smet established several missions in what is now Montana, near Missoula, and in 1847, he published a book about his travels and missions (fig. 35). De Smet played a significant role in negotiating the Fort Laramie Treaty of 1851, between the Cheyenne, Sioux, Arapahoe, Crow, Assiniboine, Mandan, Hidatsa and Arikara, on the one side, and the United States on the other. And in 1868, he persuaded the Sioux war chief Sitting Bull to accept the terms of a revised Treaty of Fort Laramie.

FARMERS AND RANCHERS

In the Treaty of Paris of 1783, which ended the Revolutionary War, Great Britain ceded to the new United States its right and title to all land it claimed from the Atlantic to the Mississippi River. The vast bulk of the Midwest was obtained from France pursuant to the Louisiana Purchase in 1803. The American Southwest became part of the United States under the terms of the Treaty of Guadalupe Hidalgo of 1848, at the conclusion of the Mexican War. However, the acquisition of the Pacific Northwest was much less straightforward. The Spanish were likely its first Europeans explorers; the Strait of Juan de Fuca and other Spanish place names appear on some early maps. However, Spain surrendered any rights it might have had in the Pacific

Northwest when it entered into the Adams-Onis Treaty of 1819, which established the American-Spanish territorial boundary in the Southwest. With that settled, this issue remained to be resolved solely between the United States and Great Britain (both ignored the claims of the Native Americans). The claim of the United States was based on several factors, including: Capt. Robert Gray's discovery of the mouth of the major river in the area, the Columbia, (named after the ship on which Gray was sailing); the westward trek by Lewis and Clark in 1804–06; and the establishment of Astoria, in 1810, by John Jacob Astor's Pacific Fur Company, a subsidiary of his American Fur Company.

The British claim was based on, among other things, the exploration of the upper reaches of the Columbia River by George Vancouver's expedition in the early 1790s; Alexander Mackenzie's trek across the Canadian Rockies and down to the Pacific in 1793; and the activities of the British fur trading companies—the Hudson's Bay Company and the North West Company—in the late eighteenth and early nineteenth centuries. Ultimately, in 1818, the United States and England agreed on joint occupation of the land. However, until the final line was drawn, England claimed everything as far south as the north bank of the Columbia River, and the United States claimed everything south of 54 degrees 40 minutes north latitude, an area that reached far into present-day British Columbia.

Although American fur trappers and traders had moved into the Pacific Northwest in the early 1800s, the British occupied almost all the settlements. By the late 1830s, it became clear that, if the United States were going to lay exclusive claim to part of that territory, Americans needed to start moving there and occupying some of the land. Initially, missionaries in the Northwest, some of them accompanied by their wives, played a big role in encouraging migration. Popular books like Samuel Parker's *Journal of an Exploring Tour Beyond the Rocky Mountains*, and lectures to potential settlers extolling the virtues of the soil and climate in places like the Willamette Valley, also helped. Emigration societies were formed and, with publications and information exchanges, encouraged both US and non-citizens alike to migrate to the Northwest.

THE OREGON TRAIL

In 1843, on a trip later known as "The Great Migration," missionary Marcus Whitman led the first group of about 1000 settlers to Oregon, along what became popularly known as the Oregon Trail. Another 1500 people made the trek the next year, and twice as many the year after that. As the population swelled, pressure began building on Congress to resolve the question of American rights in the Northwest. Finally, the Webster-Ashburton Treaty of 1846, negotiated by Daniel Webster for the United States and Lord Ashburton for Great Britain, established the northern boundary of the United States along the line of the 49th parallel of north latitude to the Pacific Ocean.

Despite the romance associated with stories of westward migration, the Oregon Trail was no picnic. Beginning in Independence, Missouri, the trail went northwest to the Platte River, at Fort Kearny (Nebraska), continuing until the river split into the North Platte and the South Platte. At that point, some parties followed the South Platte awhile, then cut across country, back to the North Platte. Others continued to follow the North Platte, where several iconic landmarks can be found: Chimney Rock, Scott's Bluff, and Independence Rock—a landmark most caravans hoped to reach by the Fourth of July. Also along the North Platte was the way station of Fort Laramie, in present-day Wyoming. (Formerly a British fur trading outpost, the United States purchased it in 1849 and renamed it after a French fur trader, Jacques La Ramie.) All parties then followed the Sweetwater River into the South Pass, the most easily traversable crossing of the Rocky Mountains.

For the first several years, all parties went southwest of the South Pass to Fort Bridger, a fur trading post established by mountain man Jim Bridger, to restock, and then proceeded northwest to Fort Hall, an American fur-trading outpost on the Snake River in present-day Idaho. After Fort Hall the route was extremely rugged, until the parties reached the Columbia River Valley, usually at the settlement called The Dalles, in what is now Oregon. Although the Oregon Trail officially ended at The Dalles, many emigrants wanted to go further down the Columbia River, to the Willamette Valley. However, going from The Dalles down the Columbia, to Fort Vancouver (located on the Columbia at the Willamette River) could be a true nightmare journey. In 1846, two entrepreneurs built a wagon road (subsequently called the Barlow Road), to allow emigrants to continue directly to Oregon City, on the Willamette, south of Fort Vancouver, without the danger and expense of the Columbia River route. In the mid-1840s, the US Senate directed Charles Preuss, a German topographer and outstanding mapmaker, who had accompanied John C. Fremont on his explorations of the West, to prepare a multi-sectioned, highly detailed map of the Oregon Trail (fig. 36).

31

WASHINGTON IRVING (1783–1859) · *SKETCH OF THE ROUTES OF HUNT & STUART*

9¾ x 17⅞ in. From: *Astoria, or Anecdotes of an Enterprise Beyond the Rocky Mountains*. Philadelphia: Carey, Lea, & Blanchard, 1836.

Short-story writer and biographer Washington Irving is more widely known as the author of *Rip Van Winkle* and *The Legend of Sleepy Hollow*. But Irving was also fascinated by western exploration, and his two-volume book was an immediate bestseller. This map shows the outbound and return routes of the Astorians in 1811 and 1812.

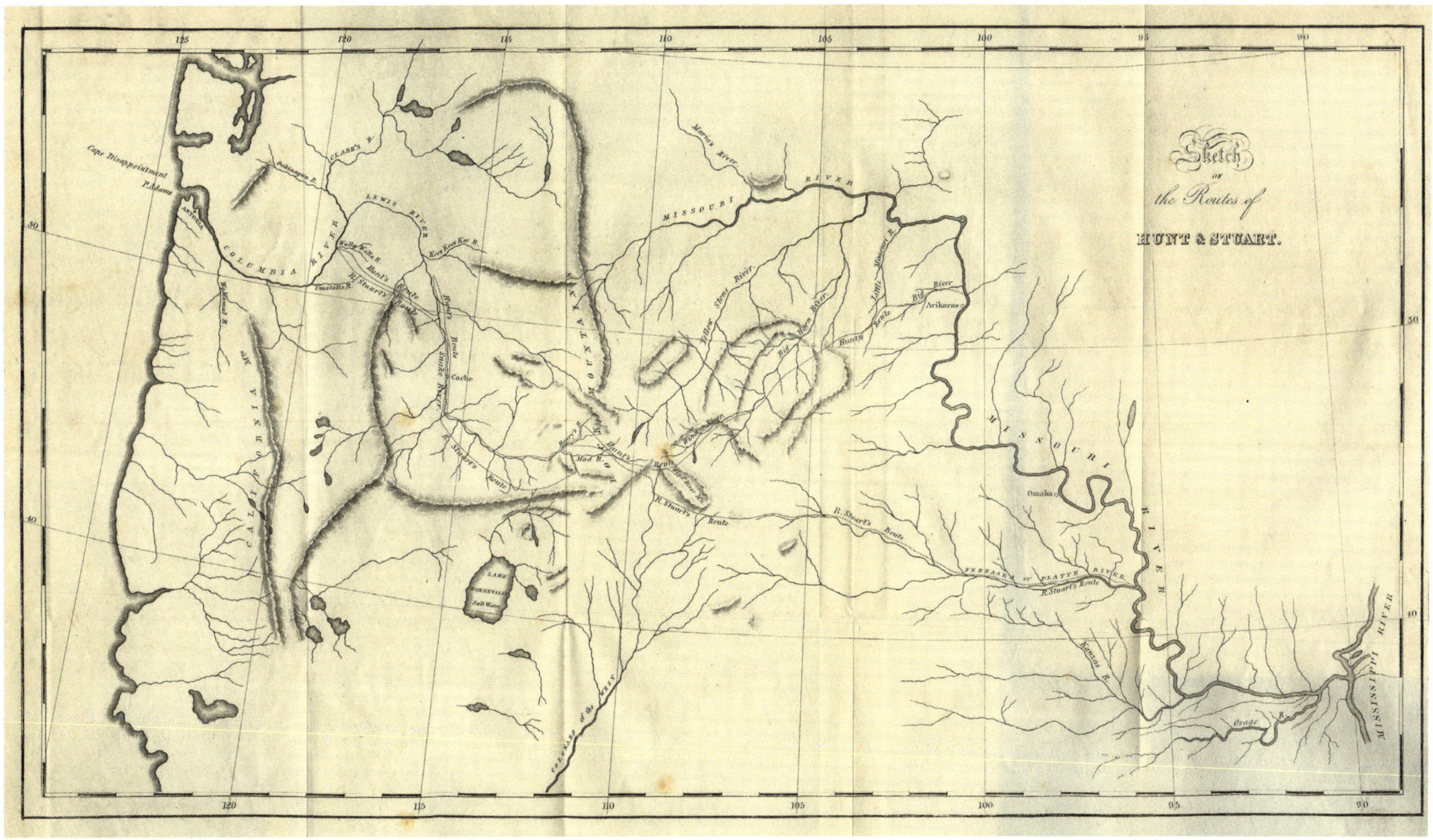

32

B. L. E. BONNEVILLE (1796-1878) · *MAP OF THE TERRITORY WEST OF THE ROCKY MOUNTAINS*

New York: S. Stiles, 1837. 17½ x 16 in. From: Washington Irving: *The Rocky Mountains: or, Scenes, Incidents, and Adventures in the Far West. Digested from the Journal of Captain B. L. E. Bonneville, of the Army of the United States, and Illustrated from Various Other Sources* (Philadelphia: Carey, Lea, & Blanchard, 1837).

Having achieved a great deal of success with his book on the expeditions to establish the first American fur trading post in the Pacific Northwest, *Astoria* (1836), Washington Irving wrote another rip-roaring travelogue, based on the adventures in the West of Army Capt. Benjamin Bonneville from 1832–35. Each of the two volumes of Irving's work contained a map. This map, by Bonneville, was said by Gouverneur K. Warren (1830–1882) of the US Army Corps of Topographical Engineers, in his *Memoir to Accompany the Map of the Territory of the United States from the Mississippi River to the Pacific Ocean* (1858), to be the first to correctly show the hydrography of the area west of the Rocky Mountains; the first to indicate that there are several large interior basins in the inter-mountain West that have no outlet to the sea; and the first to show the Great Salt Lake, and Mary's or Ogden's River (later named the Humboldt River). The map also discredited the idea of a Buenaventura River, or River of the West; shortened the Willamette River (then known as the Multonomah [*sic*] or Wallamuth River) to its true length, and determined the general direction and extent of the Sacramento and San Joaquin Rivers.

33

B. L. E. BONNEVILLE (1796–1878)

A MAP OF THE SOURCES OF THE COLORADO & BIG SALT LAKE, PLATTE, YELLOW-STONE, MUSCLE-SHELL, MISSOURI; & SALMON & SNAKE RIVERS, BRANCHES OF THE COLUMBIA RIVER

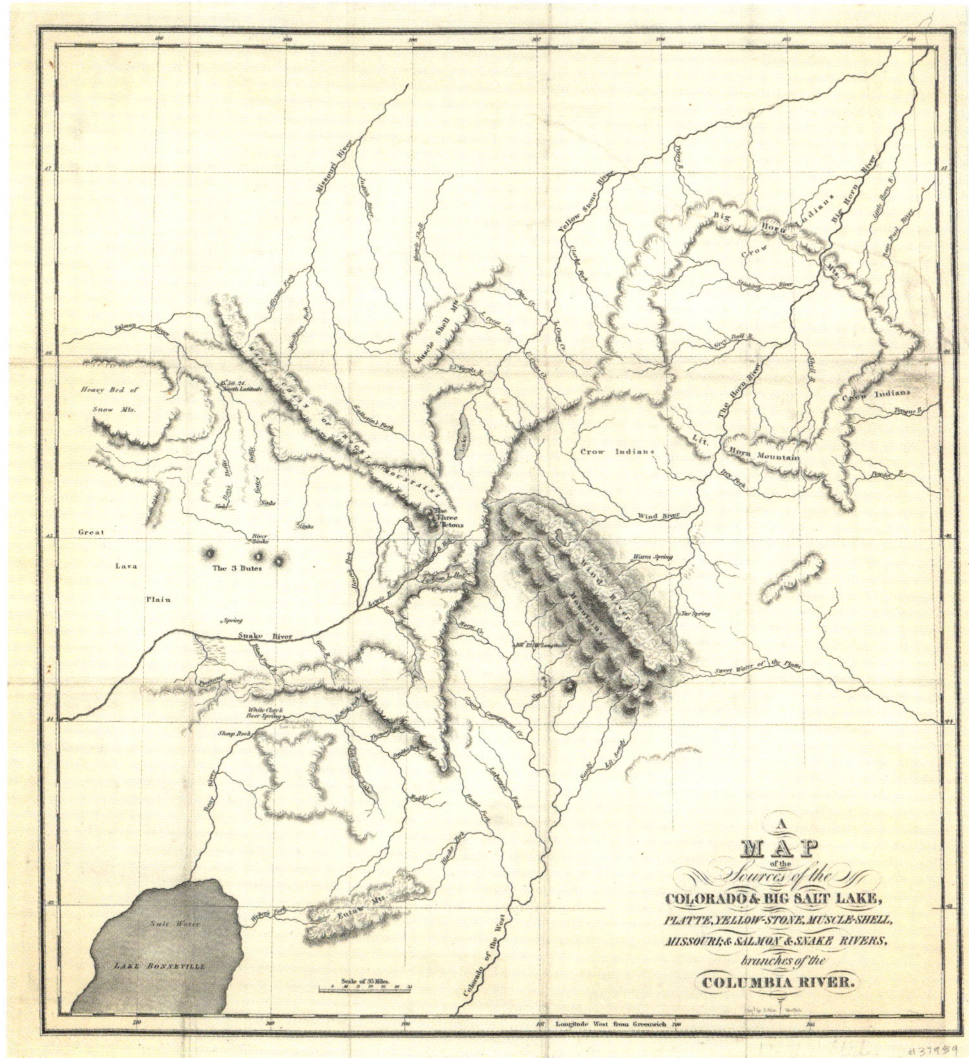

New York: S Stiles, 1837. 15⅜ x 16⅛ in. From: Washington Irving, *The Rocky Mountains: or Scenes, Incidents, and Adventures in the Far West. Digested from the Journal of Captain B. L. E. Bonneville, of the Army of the United States, and Illustrated from Various Other Sources* (Philadelphia: Carey, Lea, & Blanchard, 1837).

This map by Bonneville, according to Gouverneur Warren was, at that time, the most accurate map of the sources of the Yellowstone River.

MAP
OF
OREGON TERRITORY.
BY
Samuel Parker.
1838.
Copy right secured.
English Miles 69½ = One Degree.
Engd by M.M.Peabody. Utica N.Y.

34

SAMUEL PARKER (1779–1866) · *MAP OF OREGON TERRITORY*

Utica, NY: M. M. Peabody, 1838. 22⅜ x 14 in. From: *Journal of an Exploring Tour Beyond the Rocky Mountains, Under the Direction of the A. B. C. F. M. Performed in the Years 1835, '36 And '37* (Ithaca, NY: Published by the author, 1838).

Even though he was a minister, and not a cartographer, Parker drew an outstanding map of the Oregon Territory in 1838, eight years before the northern boundary of the United States was settled west of the Rocky Mountains by the Webster-Ashburton Treaty of 1846.

THE LODGE POLE (Indian Name.)
Great Chief of the Flat-heads.
VICTOR (in Baptism.) *Letter 24.*

OREGON MISSIONS
and Travels over the
ROCKY MOUNTAINS,
in 1845 46.

MARY QUILLE IN THE BATTLE AGAINST THE CROWS.

BY

FATHER P.J. DE SMET.

OF THE SOCIETY OF

JESUS.

NEW-YORK,
Published by Edward Dunigan.
1847.

35

PIERRE-JEAN DE SMET (1801–1873)
OREGON MISSIONS AND TRAVELS OVER THE ROCKY MOUNTAINS IN 1845–46

New York: Edward Dunigan, 1847.

De Smet's book, a travel narrative and description of the Jesuit missions in the Pacific Northwest, was popular among travelers along the Oregon Trail.

36

CHARLES PREUSS (1803–1854)

TOPOGRAPHICAL MAP OF THE ROAD FROM MISSOURI TO OREGON COMMENCING AT THE MOUTH OF THE KANSAS IN THE MISSOURI RIVER AND ENDING AT THE MOUTH OF THE WALLAH WALLAH IN THE COLUMBIA, IN VII SECTIONS . . .

Compiled by Charles Preuss, 1846, by Order of the Senate of the United States. Section IV. Baltimore: E. Weber & Co., 1846. 26 x 15¾ in.

Charles Preuss mapped much of the West. He served on several of John C. Fremont's expeditions, and mapped the Great Basin, Oregon, California and many other locations. This map, one of a seven-part set of maps, provided detailed information for travelers, and shows what beautiful drawings Preuss made.

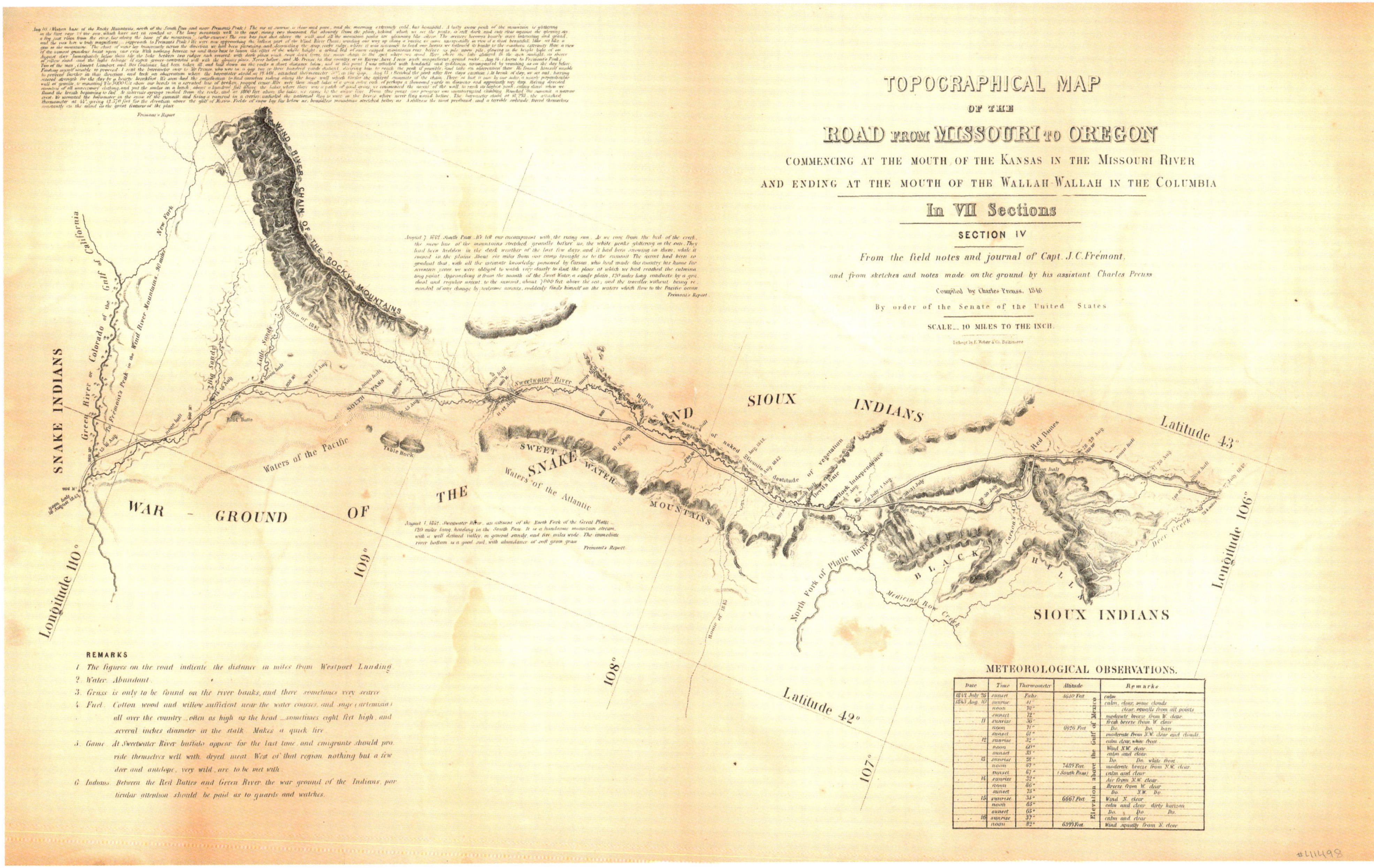

METEOROLOGICAL OBSERVATIONS.

Date	Time	Thermometer	Altitude	Remarks
1842 July 26	sunset	Fahr.	4640 Feet	calm
1843 Aug. 10	sunrise	41°		calm, clear; some clouds
	noon	76°		clear, squalls from all points
	sunset	72°		moderate breeze from W. clear
11	sunrise	36°		fresh breeze from W. clear
	noon	71°	6926 Feet	Do. Do. hazy
	sunset	61°		moderate from N.W. clear and clouds.
12	sunrise	32°		calm clear, white frost.
	noon	60°		Wind N.W. clear
	sunset	33°		calm and clear
13	sunrise	28°		Do. Do. white frost.
	noon	67°	7489 Feet	moderate breeze from N.W. clear.
	sunset	67°	(South Pass)	calm and clear
14	sunrise	32°		Air from N.W. clear.
	noon	86°		Breeze from W. clear
	sunset	75°		Do. N.W. Do.
15	sunrise	34°	6667 Feet	Wind N. clear
	noon	85°		calm and clear dirty horizon
	sunset	65°		Do. Do. Do.
16	sunrise	37°		calm and clear
	noon	82°	6399 Feet	Wind squally from N. clear

(Altitude column: Elevation above the Gulf of Mexico)

C. ZION: THE MORMONS MOVE TO UTAH

Prior to the California Gold Rush, one of the largest migrations to the West occurred in 1846 and 1847, when members of the Church of Jesus Christ of Latter-day Saints (the Mormons) traveled to the Salt Lake Valley of what is now Utah. During and after that time, Mormons also populated many places in the West, which retain large Mormon populations to this day. There are a number of explorations that are significant to Mormon history, both from the point of view of stimulating Mormon interest in the Salt Lake Valley, and in the telling of the Mormons' story. For example, one of the significant sources of information to Mormon leader Brigham Young, in deciding on a place to settle, was John C. Fremont's *Report of an Exploring Expedition to the Rocky Mountains in the Year 1842 and to Oregon and North California in the Years 1843–44.*

From the founding of the church in 1830 until the mid-1840s, Mormons sought a variety of locations in the East to practice their religion in peace. By 1844, many of them had settled in Nauvoo, Illinois, on the Mississippi River. Nearly two years after Mormon Church founder Joseph Smith was killed in Carthage, Illinois, near Nauvoo, 3000 Mormons in 500 wagons began a migration westward, along what became known as the Mormon Trail. Travel was very slow, and the vast majority of the travelers spent the winter of 1846–47 in Winter Quarters, close to the junction of the Missouri and Platte Rivers, near modern-day Omaha, Nebraska. The next April, an advance party of 148 Mormons and 72 wagons, led by Brigham Young, continued west, following the Oregon Trail, up the Platte River, then up the North Platte, through the South Pass, to Fort Bridger. Leaving the Oregon Trail, they followed a trail that had been blazed the prior autumn by the ill-fated Donner party. They crossed the Wasatch Mountains, and when they passed through what is now known as Emigration Canyon, and looked out on the Salt Lake Valley, Young declared "this is the place." In 1899, a Salt Lake City hotel issued a commemorative map of this journey (fig. 37). Much was written about the Mormons—their religion and culture—in the decades immediately after their arrival in the Inter-Mountain West. Some of those narratives were generally positive, others less so. One of the best known of those writings was a best seller authored by the prominent British adventurer and traveler Sir Richard Burton, who traveled west in 1860 and spent a great deal of time among the Mormons, chronicling their activities in words and images (fig. 38).

37

MILLROY & HAYES

ROUTE OF THE MORMON PIONEERS FROM NAUVOO TO GREAT SALT LAKE, FEB'Y 1846–JULY 1847

Salt Lake City: New Wilson European Hotel, 1899. 28¾ x 8½ in.

Although it was published over fifty years after the initial Mormon migration to the Salt Lake Valley, this map illustrates, in a pictorial fashion, many of the landmarks encountered on the journey. One of the interesting features of this map is a notation (with an illustration) of something called the "Mormon Battalion," just south of the junction of the Missouri and the Platte, at Council Bluffs, Iowa. This was a group of Mormons who, while on the way west, were conscripted by the US Army to fight in the Mexican War. They weren't too happy about it, but they acquitted themselves very well.

ISSUED BY THE NEW WILSON
GREAT SALT LAKE
UTAH LAKE
DEVIL'S SLIDE
PULPIT ROCK
BRIDGER
GIANT'S BUTTE
DEVILS GATE
INDEPENDENCE ROCK
RED BUTTES
North Platte
LARAMIE PK.
LARAMIE CITY
CHEYENNE
SCOTTSBLUFFS
CHIMNEY ROCK
DENVER
OLD TRADING POST
Denver Lith Co. Denver, Colo.
July, 1847.
ROUTE OF THE MORMON PIONEERS

PEAN HOTEL, SALT LAKE CITY
Missouri River
Elkhorn River
Platte
WINTER QUARTERS
COUNCIL BLUFFS
PLATTSMOUTH
NEW FT. KEARNEY
GRAND ISLAND
FT. DES MOINES
MONROE
DUBUQUE
BURLINGTON
NAUVOO
CARTHAGE
WARSAW
QUINCY
KEOKUK
ST. JOSEPH
FT. LEAVENWORTH
KANSAS CITY
INDEPENDENCE
MISSOURI
ST. LOUIS
Copyright 1899, By MILLROY & HAYES
OM NAUVOO TO GREAT SALT LAKE.
Feb'y, 1846.

38

SIR RICHARD FRANCIS BURTON (1821–1890)
ROUTE FROM THE MISSOURI RIVER TO THE PACIFIC

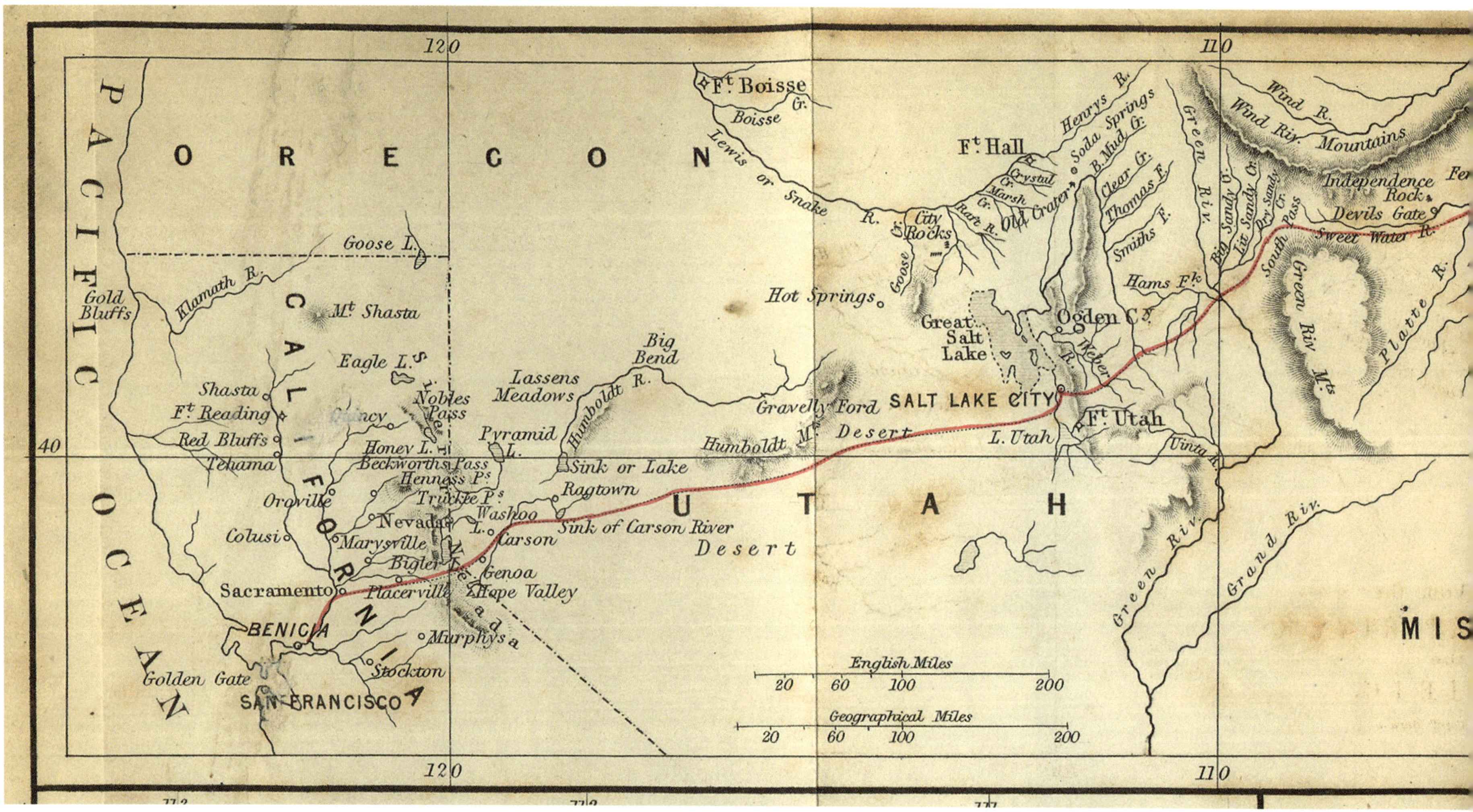

Engraved by E. Weller, 9¾ x 3¼ in. From: *The City of the Saints and Across the Rocky Mountains to California* (London: Longman, Green, Longman and Roberts, 1861).

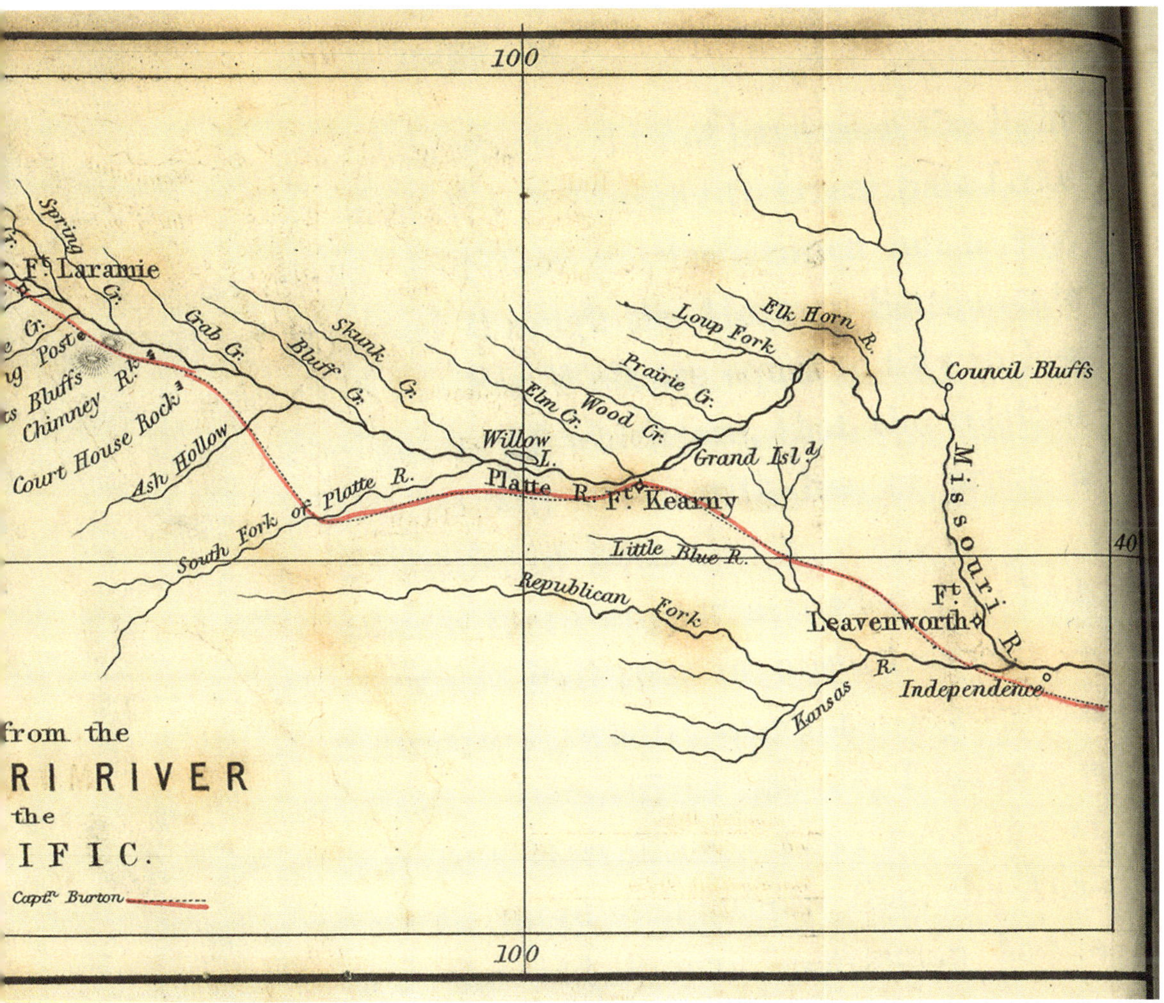

Sir Richard Burton was an English explorer, diplomat, spy, author and all-around Renaissance man. In 1860, Burton traveled across North America, spending considerable time in Salt Lake City with the Mormons. His book chronicles that journey and offers his opinions about the Latter-day Saints. The book contains a map showing Burton's route along what had, by 1860, become known as The Mormon Trail, as far as Salt Lake City, and then on to California.

D. CALIFORNIA AND NEVADA: MINING FOR GOLD AND SILVER

THE DISCOVERY OF GOLD IN CALIFORNIA

In late January 1848, James W. Marshall, a carpenter hired by John Sutter to build a sawmill for him on California's American River, discovered a small amount of gold in the mill race of the sawmill he was building. Though Marshall and Sutter were convinced that the find was significant, they tried to keep it a secret until the sawmill was completed. That didn't work, and the area soon began to flood with prospectors for gold. In July of 1848, Col. R. B. Mason, the military commander of California, took a tour through the gold regions (accompanied by, among others, Capt. William Tecumseh Sherman) and reported to his superior, General Jones, the Adjutant General of the United States Army, in a letter dated August 17, 1848:

> *We reached San Francisco on the 20th (of June) and found that all, or nearly all, of its male population had gone to the mines. The town, which a few months before was so busy and thriving, was then almost deserted . . . The discovery of these vast deposits of gold has entirely changed the character of Upper California. Its people, before engaged in cultivating their small patches of ground, and guarding their herds of cattle and horses, have all gone to the mines, or are on their way thither. Labourers of every trade have left their work-benches, and tradesmen their shops; sailors desert their ships as fast as they arrive on the coast; and several vessels have gone to sea with hardly enough hands to spread a sail . . . Many desertions, too, have taken place from the garrisons within the influence of the mines . . .*[10]

This report was accompanied by several maps, drawn by personnel who accompanied Colonel Mason, and represented perhaps the earliest maps of the region of the California Gold Rush (figs. 39, 40 and 42).

Nothing changed the West as much as the discovery of gold in California. One source has indicated that there were 1800 emigrants to California in 1846. By 1849, there were 41,000, and in 1850, there were 60,000. A substantial number of these fortune seekers came around Cape Horn, and many used land routes other than the traditional California Trail. Despite the fact that the fate of the Donner party in 1846 and 1847 was quickly and graphically told (fig. 41), prospectors didn't hesitate to pour across the route the Donner party had disastrously taken. Not surprisingly, numerous narratives and maps about how to get to California and where to find gold were issued (fig. 43), as well as publications on the best type of equipment for gold mining and detailed maps of the prime areas to prospect for gold.

---

10. Letter from Col. R. B. Mason to General R. Jones, Adjutant General, U. S. A., August 17, 1848, in *Message from the President of the United States Transmitting Information in Answer to a Resolution of the House of the 31st of December, 1849, on the subject of California and New Mexico, 31st Cong. 1st Sess., Ho. of Reps. Ex. Doc. No. 17, January 24, 1850*, pp. 528–36.

THE DISCOVERY OF PRECIOUS METALS ELSEWHERE IN THE WEST

Once it became apparent that there was not enough gold in California to enrich all the prospectors, people began to move on, seeking other opportunities. In fact, Colonel Mason observed in his 1848 report on the California gold fields that nearly all the Mormons were leaving California for the Great Salt Lake area because it had been reported that gold had been discovered there.

In the 1850s, a small group of placer miners panned for gold in the Virginia Range, northeast of the Carson Valley, in what is now Nevada. Some were moderately successful. In 1859, others recovered gold in that same area, on the northwest slopes of Mount Davidson, and in an area called Gold Canyon, two miles south. Though gold was what brought the prospectors to the area in the first place, it soon became apparent that silver (which was originally thought to be a nuisance blue clay) was by far the most valuable metal in the ground. The discovery was named the Comstock Lode, not because Henry Comstock had discovered it, but because he claimed to own the land on which it was found (fig. 44).

This discovery led to the "Rush to Washoe," and to the almost immediate establishment of several new Nevada towns, including Virginia City, Gold Hill and Silver City. The residents of this incredibly rich, and rapidly growing, silver and gold mining area were located in the far western part of the Utah Territory, some 500 miles from Salt Lake City. They were unwilling to be governed by the Utah Territorial government, so in the early 1860s, they petitioned Washington to become a separate territory, and then a state. What became Nevada was full of ex-Californians and New Yorkers.

Also in the early 1860s, German immigrant Adolph Sutro arrived in Virginia City from the California gold fields. He proposed to build an ore milling operation near the Carson River to eliminate the costs of shipping the ore out for processing. Later in the 1860s, he proposed to dig a four-mile long tunnel, from near the river, into the base of Mt. Davidson. The tunnel would penetrate the ore bodies at considerable depth, drain water from the mines, and provide greater ventilation in the mine shafts and rooms. The tunnel was completed in 1878, 1600 feet below Virginia City (fig. 45). Unfortunately, the lode had, by that time, been played out, and Sutro sold his interest in the tunnel, invested in San Francisco real estate and was later elected mayor of San Francisco.

In 1858, gold was discovered in Colorado, and more than 100,000 people flooded into that area. In November 1858, the town of Denver was founded on land which had been promised to the Arapahoe and Cheyenne Indians in the 1851 Treaty of Fort Laramie. Precious metals were discovered in Idaho and Montana in the 1860s, and in the Black Hills of South Dakota, an area sacred to the Sioux, in the 1870s.

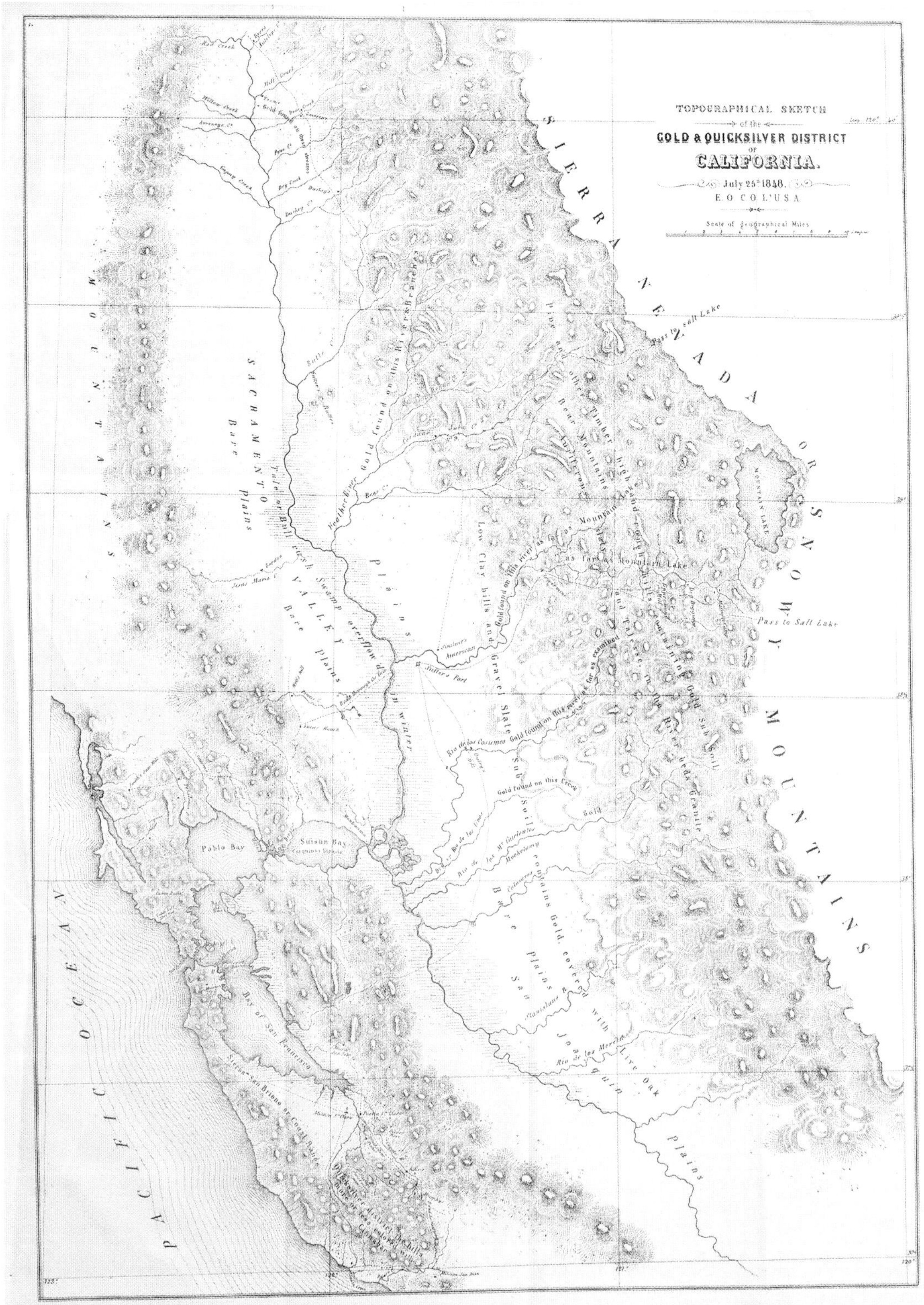
TOPOGRAPHICAL SKETCH
of the
GOLD & QUICKSILVER DISTRICT
OF
CALIFORNIA.
July 25th 1848.
E. O. C. O. L.'U.S.A.
Scale of Geographical Miles
SIERRA NEVADA OR SNOWY MOUNTAINS
MOUNTAINS
PACIFIC OCEAN
SACRAMENTO Bare Plains
VALLEY Bare Plains
Pablo Bay
Suisun Bay
Bay of San Francisco
Pass to Salt Lake
Sutter's Fort
Mountain Lake
Plains
Low Clay hills and Gravel Slate
Gold found on this Creek
Bare Plains San Joaquin
Stanislaus R.
Rio de los Merced
Rio de los Cosumnes
Live Oak

39

E. O. C. ORD (1818–1883)
TOPOGRAPHICAL SKETCH OF THE GOLD AND QUICKSILVER DISTRICT OF CALIFORNIA, JULY 25TH, 1848 [to accompany R. B. Mason's Report]

Philadelphia: P. S. Duval's Lith. Steam Press, 1848. 15⅜ x 21½ in. From: 30th Cong., 2nd Sess., House Ex. Doc. No. 1 (Washington, DC, 1848).

Edward Ord was a young West Point graduate when he was sent to California during the Mexican War, in 1847, with his classmates Henry Halleck and William Tecumseh Sherman. In January of 1848, gold was discovered at Sutter's Mill. In June and July of that year, Col. R. B. Mason, the military governor of California, conducted a fact-finding tour of the gold fields, accompanied by Ord and Sherman. The map that Ord sent back to Washington with Mason's report was one of the first to show the extent of the gold fields, and helped to trigger the California gold rush.

40

WILLIAM T. SHERMAN (1820–1891)

POSITIONS OF THE UPPER AND LOWER GOLD MINES ON THE SOUTH FORK OF THE AMERICAN RIVER, CALIFORNIA, JULY 20, 1848 [to accompany R. B. Mason's Report]

Philadelphia: P. S. Duval's Lith. Steam Press, 1848. 9¼ x 18¼ in. From: 30th Cong., 2nd Sess., House Ex. Doc. No. 1 (Washington, DC, 1848).

Sherman, who accompanied Col. R. B. Mason and Edward Ord on Mason's tour in 1848 of the California gold mining area along the American, Russian and Sacramento Rivers, drew several large scale maps of portions of the region. Along with Ord's map, these maps accompanied Mason's report to Washington, and whetted the appetites of the '49ers.

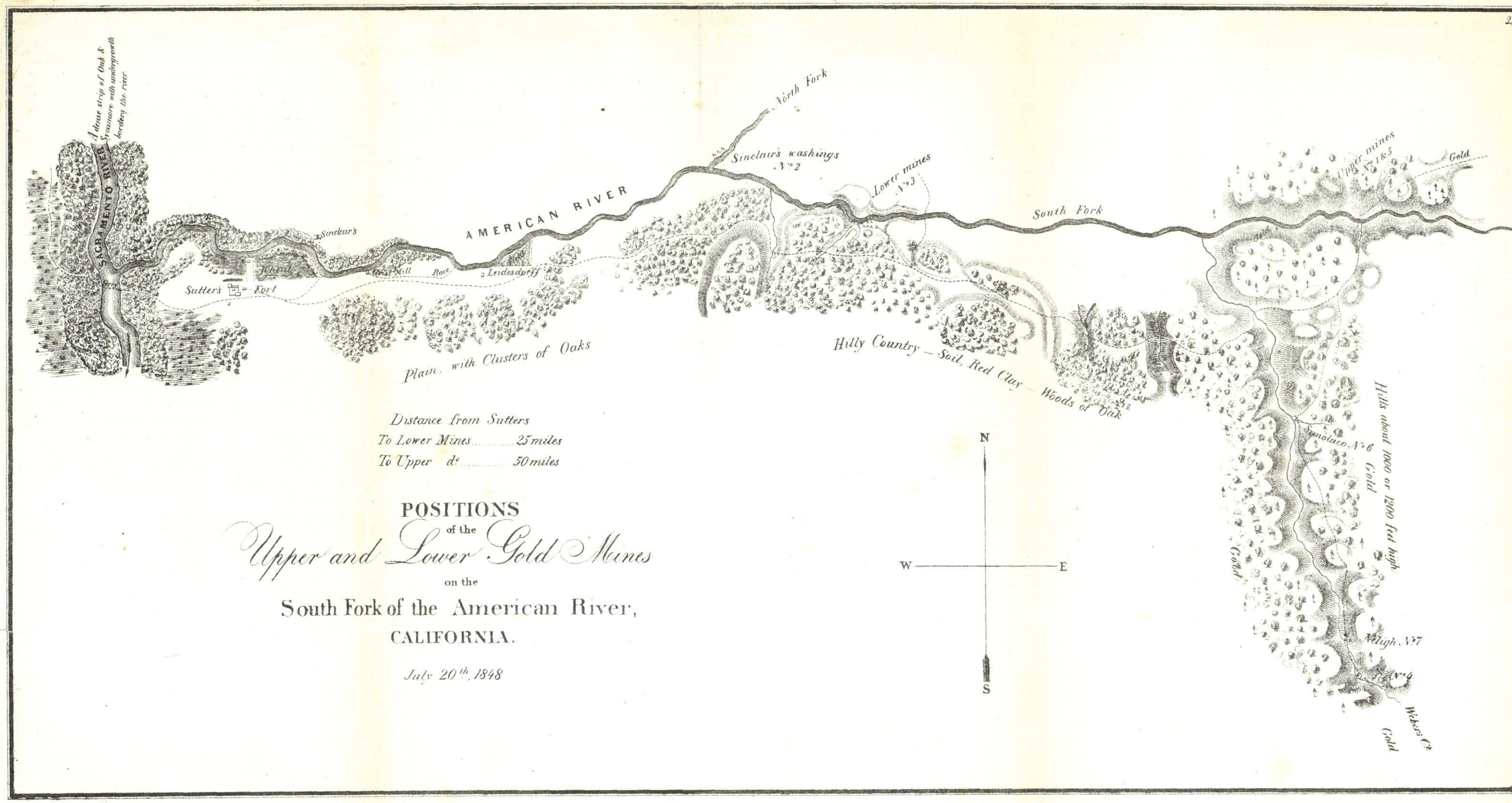
23.
A dense strip of Oak & Sycamore with undergrowth bordering the river
SACRAMENTO RIVER
Sinclair's
Sutter's Fort
AMERICAN RIVER
Leidesdorff
North Fork
Sinclair's washings
No. 2
Lower mines
No. 3
South Fork
Upper mines
Gold
Plain, with Clusters of Oaks
Hilly Country – Soil, Red Clay – Woods of Oak
Hills about 1000 or 1200 feet high
Gold
Gold
Distance from Sutters
To Lower Mines.........25 miles
To Upper do...........50 miles
POSITIONS
of the
Upper and Lower Gold Mines
on the
South Fork of the American River,
CALIFORNIA.
July 20th, 1848
N
W
E
S
Weber's Ck
Gold

41

J. HALPIN · *THE CAMP OF DEATH*

New York: Bobbett & Edmonds, 1848. Lithograph, 5 x 3 in. From: J. Quinn Thornton: *Oregon and California in 1848: With an Appendix, including Recent and Authoritative Information on the Subject of the Gold Mines of California, and Other Valuable Matter of Interest to the Emigrant, etc., with Illustrations and a Map,* Vol. II (New York: Harper & Brothers, 1849, 2 vols).

The second edition of J. Quinn Thornton's work, *Oregon and California in 1848*, published in 1849, featured a map that outlined the California Gold Regions in gold. In this book, Thornton also was one of the first to describe the fate of the Donner party during the winter of 1846–47. Despite the horrific story of the Donner party, greed overcame fear, and the route used by the Donners became one of the main routes into California less than two years later, during the gold rush.

THE CAMP OF DEATH.

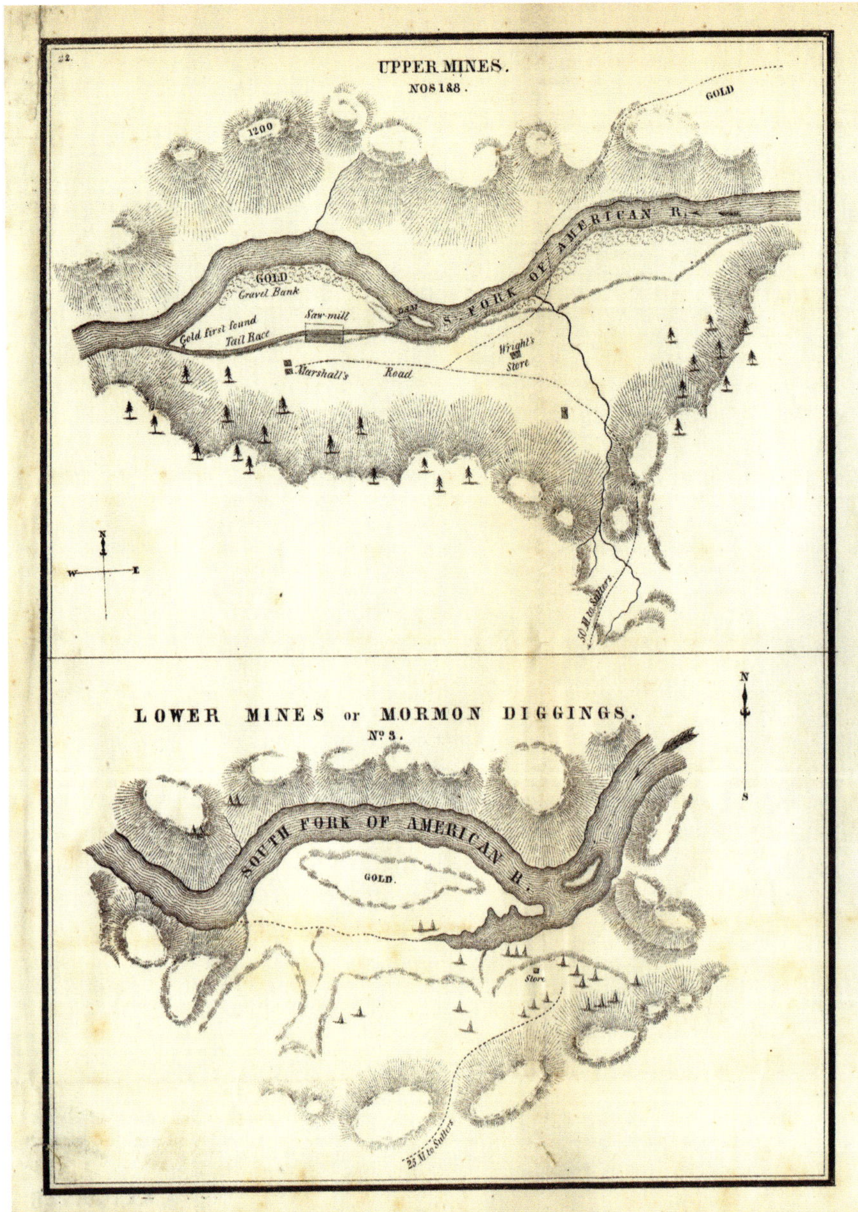

42

WILLIAM T. SHERMAN (1820–1891)
UPPER MINES NOS. 1 & 8 AND *LOWER MINES OR MORMON DIGGINGS NO. 3*

[to accompany R. B. Mason's Report]

Philadelphia: P. S. Duval's Lith. Steam Press, 1848. 9 x 6½ in. From: 30th Cong. 2nd Sess., House Ex. Doc. No. 1 (Washington, DC, 1848).

These maps accompanied Mason's Report to Washington (see figs. 39 and 40), and his description of the gold fields became a part of the basis for the subsequent worldwide gold rush to California.

43

JOSEPH WARREN REVERE (1812–1880) · *SUTTER'S FORT – NEW HELVETIA*

New York: Wm. Endicott & Co., 1849. Lithograph, 6 x 9 in. From: Joseph Warren Revere: *A Tour of Duty in California; including a Description of the Gold Regions and an Account of the Voyage Around Cape Horn* (New York: C. S. Francis & Co., 1849).

Revere was a grandson of Paul Revere, who used his time while stationed in California with the US Army to great advantage by writing a bestselling book which described the gold country and how to get there.

44

GRAFTON TYLER BROWN (1841–1918)
MAP OF THE LOWER COMSTOCK AND EMIGRANT CONSOLIDATED MINING COS. MINES, LYON COUNTY, NEV.

San Francisco: G. T. Brown & Co., 1866. 15½ x 7½ in.

This is an early map of the claims of the Comstock Lode, done by one of the first African-American lithographers in the West.

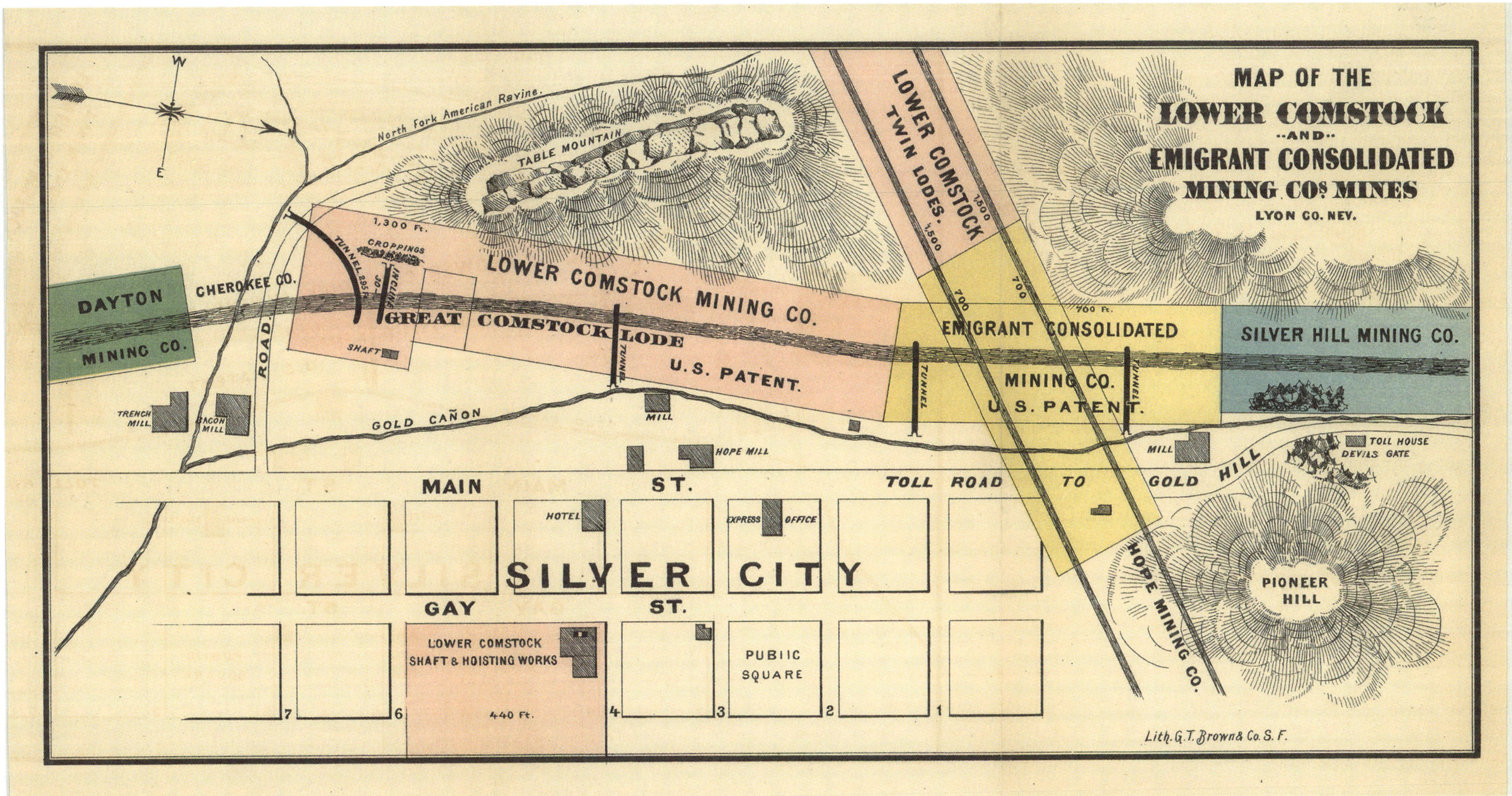
MAP OF THE
LOWER COMSTOCK
--AND--
EMIGRANT CONSOLIDATED
MINING CO'S MINES
LYON CO. NEV.
North Fork American Ravine.
TABLE MOUNTAIN
LOWER COMSTOCK TWIN LODES.
1,300 Ft.
CROPPINGS
TUNNEL 285 Ft.
INCLINE
DAYTON MINING CO.
CHEROKEE CO.
LOWER COMSTOCK MINING CO.
GREAT COMSTOCK LODE
U.S. PATENT.
SHAFT
TUNNEL
ROAD.
EMIGRANT CONSOLIDATED MINING CO. U.S. PATENT.
700 Ft.
SILVER HILL MINING CO.
TRENCH MILL
BACON MILL
GOLD CAÑON
MILL
HOPE MILL
TOLL HOUSE
DEVILS GATE
MAIN ST.
TOLL ROAD TO GOLD HILL
HOTEL
EXPRESS OFFICE
SILVER CITY
GAY ST.
HOPE MINING CO.
PIONEER HILL
LOWER COMSTOCK SHAFT & HOISTING WORKS
440 Ft.
PUBIIC SQUARE
Lith. G.T. Brown & Co. S.F.

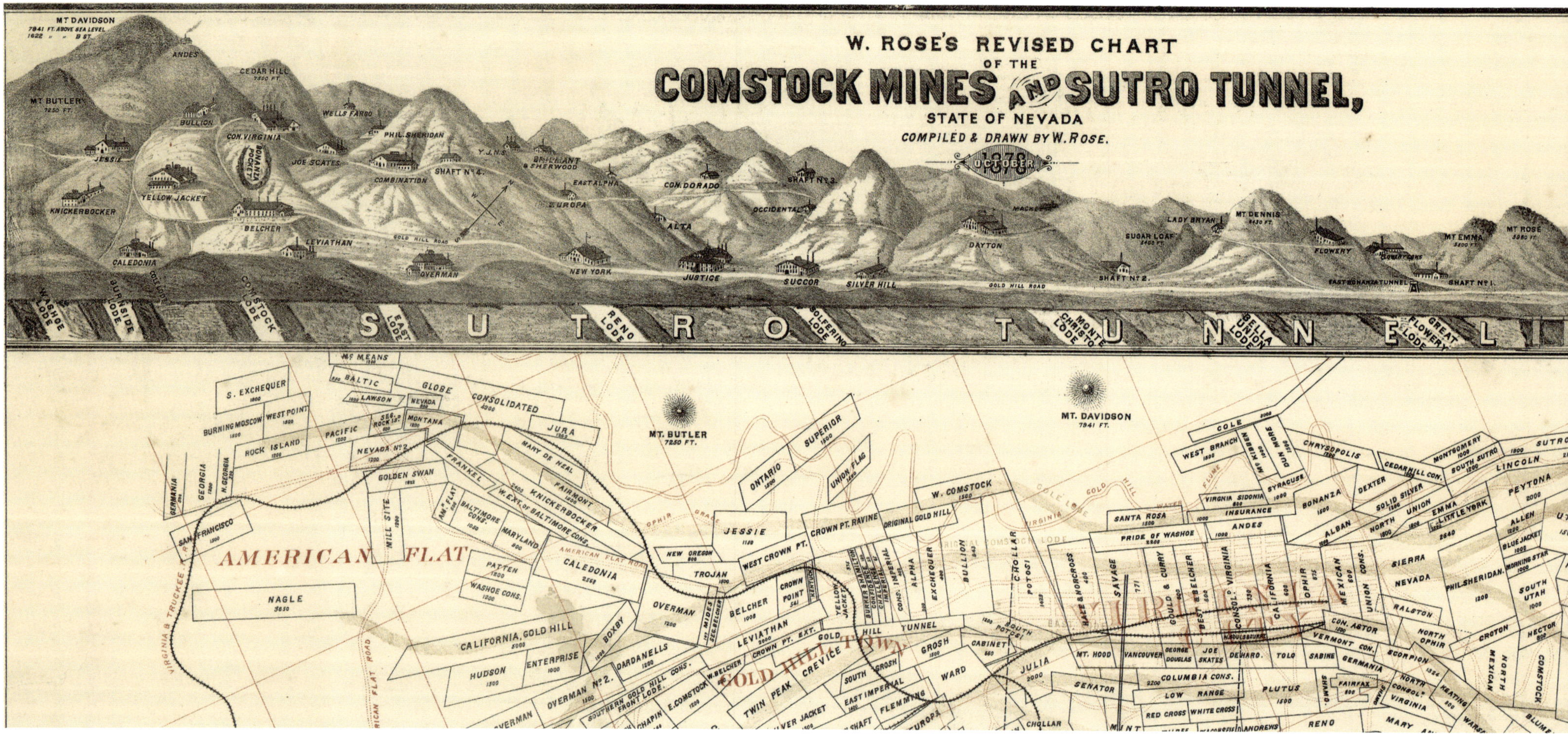
W. ROSE'S REVISED CHART
OF THE
COMSTOCK MINES AND SUTRO TUNNEL,
STATE OF NEVADA
COMPILED & DRAWN BY W. ROSE.
OCTOBER
MT. DAVIDSON
MT. BUTLER
ANDES
CEDAR HILL
BULLION
CON. VIRGINIA
BONANZA POCKET
WELLS FARGO
PHIL. SHERIDAN
JESSIE
JOE SCATES
YELLOW JACKET
KNICKERBOCKER
COMBINATION
SHAFT No. 4.
BELCHER
LEVIATHAN
CALEDONIA
OVERMAN
EUROPA
ALTA
CON. DORADO
OCCIDENTAL
SHAFT No. 3.
NEW YORK
JUSTICE
SUCCOR
SILVER HILL
GOLD HILL ROAD
DAYTON
SHAFT No. 2.
SUGAR LOAF
LADY BRYAN
MT. DENNIS
FLOWERY
MT. EMMA
MT. ROSE
SHAFT No. 1.
WARNE LODE
BURNSIDE LODE
COMSTOCK LODE
EAST LODE
RENO LODE
SOLFERINO LODE
MONTE CHRISTO LODE
BELLA UNION LODE
GREAT FLOWERY LODE
SUTRO TUNNEL
S. EXCHEQUER
BALTIC
GLOBE
LAWSON
CONSOLIDATED
BURNING MOSCOW
WEST POINT
PACIFIC
MONTANA
JURA
ROCK ISLAND
NEVADA No. 2
MARY DE NEAL
GEORGIA
GERMANIA
GOLDEN SWAN
FRANKEL
FAIRMONT
KNICKERBOCKER
W. EXT. OF BALTIMORE CONS.
SAN FRANCISCO
MILL SITE
BALTIMORE CONS.
MARYLAND
AMERICAN FLAT
PATTEN
CALEDONIA
WASHOE CONS.
NAGLE
ONTARIO
SUPERIOR
UNION FLAG
W. COMSTOCK
JESSIE
NEW OREGON
TROJAN
WEST CROWN PT.
CROWN PT. RAVINE
ORIGINAL GOLD HILL
OVERMAN
BELCHER
CROWN POINT
YELLOW JACKET
IMPERIAL
ALPHA
EXCHEQUER
BULLION
CHOLLAR
POTOSI
CALIFORNIA, GOLD HILL
BOXBY
LEVIATHAN
CROWN PT. EXT.
GOLD HILL TUNNEL
GOLD HILL TOWN
HUDSON
ENTERPRISE
DARDANELLS
OVERMAN No. 2.
SOUTHERN GOLD HILL CONS.
FRONT LODE.
E. COMSTOCK
W. BELCHER
TWIN PEAK
CREVICE
SOUTH
GROSH
EAST IMPERIAL
WARD
CABINET
JULIA
FLEMMING
EUROPA
CHOLLAR
SOUTH POTOSI
MT. BUTLER 7250 FT.
MT. DAVIDSON 7941 FT.
COLE
WEST BRANCH
MC KIBBEN
DUN MORE
CHRYSOPOLIS
SANTA ROSA
PRIDE OF WASHOE
INSURANCE
ANDES
SYRACUSE
BONANZA
DEXTER
CEDARHILL CON.
SOLID SILVER
MONTGOMERY
SOUTH SUTRO
SUTRO
LINCOLN
PEYTONA
ALLEN
HALE & NORCROSS
SAVAGE
GOULD & CURRY
BEST & BELCHER
CONSOLD. VIRGINIA
CALIFORNIA
OPHIR
MEXICAN
UNION CONS.
ALBAN
NORTH
UNION
EMMA
LITTLE YORK
SIERRA NEVADA
PHIL. SHERIDAN
SOUTH UTAH
RALSTON
MT. HOOD
VANCOUVER
GEORGE DOUGLAS
JOE SCATES
DEHARO.
TOLO
SABINE
CON. ASTOR
VERMONT CON.
GERMANIA
SCORPION
NORTH OPHIR
CROTON
HECTOR
NORTH MEXICAN
COMSTOCK
SENATOR
COLUMBIA CONS.
LOW RANGE
RED CROSS
WHITE CROSS
PLUTUS
FAIRFAX
NORTH CONSOL. VIRGINIA
HEATING
RENO
VIRGINIA CITY
VIRGINIA & TRUCKEE
AMERICAN FLAT ROAD

45

W. ROSE

[Detail from:] *REVISED CHART OF THE COMSTOCK MINES AND SUTRO TUNNEL, STATE OF NEVADA*

San Francisco: Payot, Upham & Co. 1878. 34½ x 28 in.

This birds-eye view shows many of the claims that had been staked around the area of the original Comstock claim.

V

GETTING FROM HERE TO THERE: PLANNING FOR A TRANSCONTINENTAL RAILROAD

PRELIMINARY EFFORTS

RAILROADS had been springing up all over the East and the Midwest from their first rollout in the US in 1829. By the early 1840s, pressure began to mount for the construction of a railroad to the West Coast (though at that point, land on the West Coast south of the 42nd parallel belonged to Mexico, and land north of the 42nd parallel was jointly occupied with Great Britain). The first such suggestion may have appeared in an Ann Arbor, Michigan newspaper in 1832.[11] In 1845, one of this proposed project's greatest early supporters, Asa Whitney, petitioned Congress for the construction of a transcontinental railroad that would extend from Lake Michigan to the Columbia River (fig. 46). Though he was so vocal that he was ultimately ignored, his proposal to finance this undertaking by granting builders a certain amount of land on each side of the tracks as rights-of-way became, with some modifications, the financing method.

In 1846, the United States and Great Britain agreed that the northern boundary of the US, from Lake of the Woods (bordering Minnesota) to the Pacific Ocean would be the 49th parallel of north latitude. And with the end of the Mexican War in 1848, the United States took over the southwest area from the Rio Grande to the Pacific. As a result of all these events, and the California Gold Rush, there was almost universal agreement by the late 1840s on the need for a railroad to the Pacific coast. However, there was much disagreement about where such a railroad would begin or terminate. In addition, the concept of the "Great American Desert," perpetuated by explorers like Zebulon Pike and Stephen Long, and on maps since the 1820s, discouraged some. The very high mountains also presented a challenge and, of course, politicians wanted the line to begin, pass through or end at their favored locations.

One such politician was Missouri senator Thomas Hart Benton, who wanted a route from St. Louis to San Francisco. Benton dispatched his son-in-law, John C. Fremont, to find such a route. Fremont went along the 38th parallel, up the Arkansas River, and crossed the Sangre de Cristo Moun-

11. George Leslie Albright, *Official Explorations for Pacific Railroads 1853–1855* (Berkeley: University of California Press, 1921), 7–8.

tains into the San Luis Valley of present-day Colorado. Although Fremont encountered fierce winter storms and lost ten members of his expedition to the cold and snow, he nonetheless extolled the virtues of a 38th parallel route for a railroad.

By 1848, however, support had begun to build for a more southern route for a railroad. Reasons for that shift included fewer mountains to overcome, a warmer climate and recent acquisitions of land following the end of the Mexican War. By this time, advocates of specific routes, including the prominent architect Robert Mills (who designed the Washington Monument) petitioned Congress to consider their proposals (fig. 47).

INITIAL EXPLORATIONS

By 1849, the pressure to map out a transcontinental railroad route forced the commanding officer of the Corps of Topographical Engineers to send parties into the field to explore possible alternatives. Consistent with contemporary sentiment, the first forays were along southern routes. That year, Capt. Randolph B. Marcy was dispatched to map a route from Fort Smith, Arkansas to Santa Fe. The expedition went out the Canadian River, across the Llano Estacado (Staked Plain) of Texas, to what is now Tucumcari, New Mexico. The group then crossed the Pecos River at Anton Chico and rode on into Santa Fe. Returning, they crossed the Rio Grande at Doña Ana, went south of the Llano Estacado, to Big Spring and Fort Washita (fig.48).

Also in 1849, a lieutenant in the Corps of Topographical Engineers, James Hervey Simpson, reported that there was a good railroad route from the Rio Grande, west through the country of the Zuni Indians, across the Colorado River and into California (fig. 49). Following this recommendation, Capt. Lorenzo Sitgreaves was dispatched to explore the possible route more extensively, and to offer a second opinion. Sitgreaves went west from the Rio Grande, down the Gila River, past Fort Yuma (in present-day Arizona), across the Colorado, to Needles, California and thence to Los Angeles. Sitgreaves didn't approve of the route and said so in his report. Sitgreaves's report also went into great detail about the culture (fig. 50) and customs (fig. 51) of the Native American tribes encountered by the expedition. Despite the fact that he thought this route was incredibly difficult for emigrants, due to hostile natives, lack of water, rough terrain and no wood, it ultimately became the route for the Santa Fe Railroad.

At this time, the 38th parallel interests in Congress began to agitate for additional work to be done on their proposed route. As a result, also in 1849, Capt. Howard Stansbury of the Corps of Topographical Engineers was sent out to see if a railroad route could be surveyed across the Wasatch Mountains, and past Salt Lake City and the Great Salt Lake. Stansbury was assisted throughout by another engineer, Lt. John W. Gunnison. The party started out on May 31, 1849, and went over the usual emigrant road from Fort Leavenworth to the Platte, near Fort Kearny (now Nebraska). They then went up the South and North Forks of the Platte, to Fort Laramie, up to the Sweetwater River, and then traced it to its source at South Pass. Following the Big Sandy River to its mouth, they crossed the Green River and proceeded to Fort Bridger. Gunnison and the main part of the expedition went on to Great Salt Lake City via the Mormon Road. Stansbury and Maj. James Bridger left Fort Bridger and tried to find a better route to the Great Salt Lake (fig. 52), meeting Gunnison in Great Salt Lake City.

That fall, Stansbury went west to explore the western part of what is now Utah (fig. 53). Gunnison surveyed the Great Salt Lake and Utah Valley and wrote a history of the Mormons, including illustrations of Salt Lake City (fig. 54). On the way back east the next year, Stansbury attempted to locate a better route than the Oregon Trail from Fort Bridger, through the South Pass and down the Sweetwater River Valley. Stansbury went northeast from Salt Lake City, and across present-day southern Wyoming. That route, later known as the Overland Trail, was used by the Overland Stage Company. The routes Stansbury explored, though ignored for a long time, essentially formed a part of the ultimate route of the Union Pacific Railroad.

46

ASA WHITNEY (1797–1872)

[WHITNEY'S MAP OF PROPOSED ROUTE FROM LAKE MICHIGAN TO THE PACIFIC]

$15\frac{7}{8}$ x $9\frac{3}{8}$ in. From: *Memorial of A. Whitney, Praying a Grant of Public Land to Enable Him to Construct a Railroad from Lake Michigan to the Pacific Ocean*, 29th Cong., 1st Sess., Senate Doc. No. 161 (Washington, DC: Ritchie & Heiss, 1846).

Asa Whitney was one of the very early proponents of a transcontinental railroad. On a trip to China in the early 1840s, he became convinced that such a railroad was critical to American trade. Soon thereafter, he began petitioning Congress to fund such a project. Whitney's 1846 *Memorial*, addressed to Congress, was accompanied by this map, which actually showed only a proposed railroad route between Prairie du Chein (Wisconsin) and the South Pass. However, his proposal for a northern railroad route, from the area of Lake Michigan to Puget Sound, would ultimately be realized, when the Northern Pacific and the Great Northern Railroads crossed the northern tier.

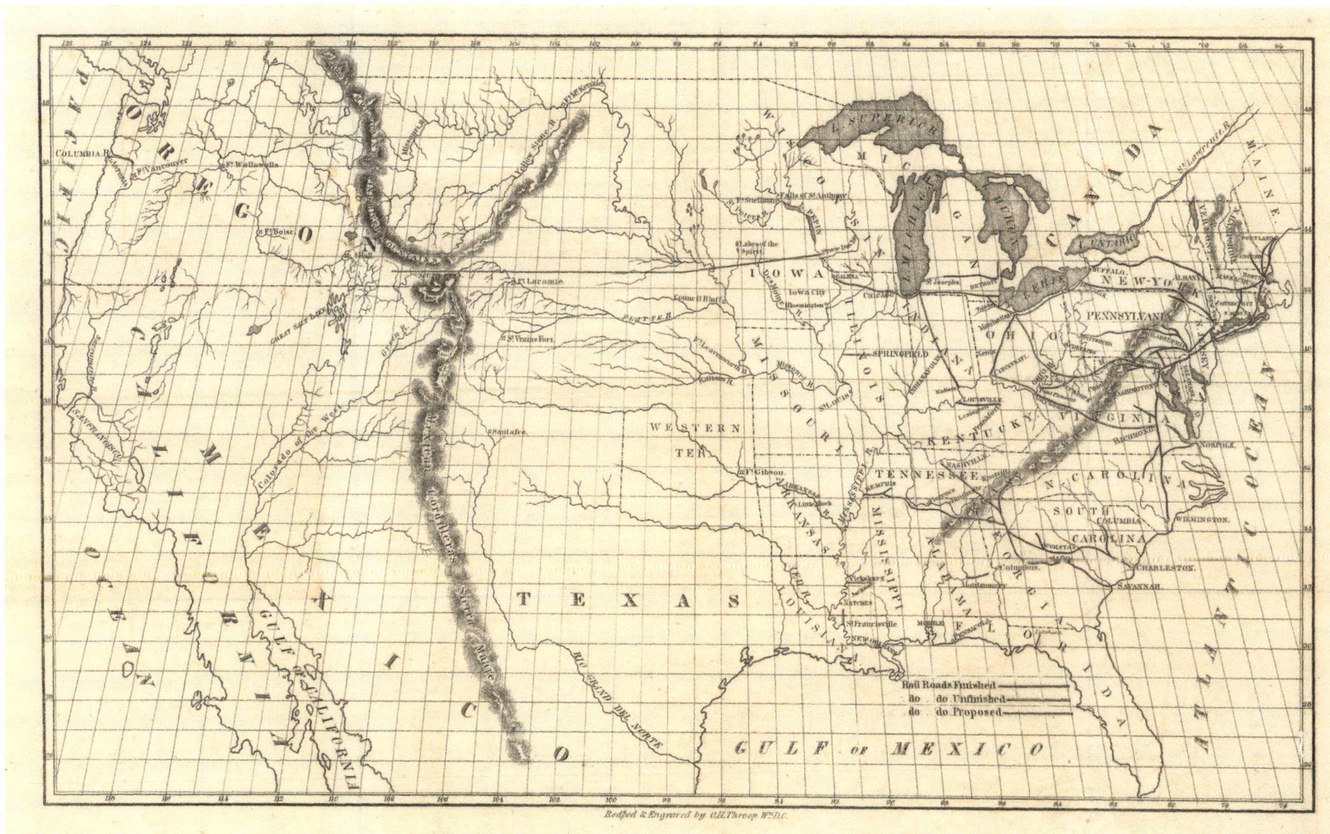

⁂ 47 ⁂

ROBERT MILLS (1781–1855)
MILLS' MAP OF THE SEVERAL ROUTES PROPOSED TO THE PACIFIC OCEAN FROM THE HEAD WATERS OF THE MISSOURI, TO THE ISTHMUS OF DARIEN

Baltimore: E. Weber & Co., 1848. 8⅞ x 8¼ in. From: *Memorial of Robert Mills, Respecting a New Route to the Pacific Ocean, with a Plan for the Transportation of Despatches to Astoria in Fifteen Days, February 15, 1848*, 30th Cong., 1st Sess., Senate Misc. No. 51 (Baltimore: E. Weber & Co., 1848).

Robert Mills, a very well known architect who designed the US Treasury building and the Washington Monument, among many other structures, submitted a proposal to Congress that showed several possible railroad routes to the West Coast. Interestingly, Mills's own proposed route ended in Mexico. His proposal for the transport of dispatches to the West Coast in fifteen days was overtaken by the completion of the transcontinental telegraph in 1861.

48

RANDOLPH B. MARCY (1812–1887) · *MAP OF THE COUNTRY BETWEEN THE FRONTIERS OF ARKANSAS AND NEW MEXICO, EMBRACING THE SECTION EXPLORED IN 1849, 50, 51, & 52, BY CAPT. R. B. MARCY 5TH U. S. INFY. UNDER ORDERS FROM THE WAR DEPARTMENT. ALSO, A CONTINUATION OF THE EMIGRANT ROAD FROM FORT SMITH AND FULTON DOWN THE VALLEY OF THE GILA.*

New York: Ackerman Lith. 1853. 59½ x 27½ in. From: *Exploration of the Red River of Louisiana, in the Year 1852 by Randolph B. Marcy, Assisted by George B. McClellan*, 32nd Cong., 2nd Sess., Senate Ex. Doc. No. 54, Serial 666 (Washington, DC: Robert Armstrong, 1853).

Randolph Marcy was a West Point graduate who fought in the Mexican War and was then stationed in Texas. He was assigned the task of finding the sources of the Red River of Texas, a goal that had eluded numerous other explorers. During his search, he mapped large parts of Texas and New Mexico, and this map is one of his most comprehensive. George McClellan, Marcy's assistant during this project, married Marcy's daughter and, during the Civil War, Marcy served as McClellan's chief of staff.

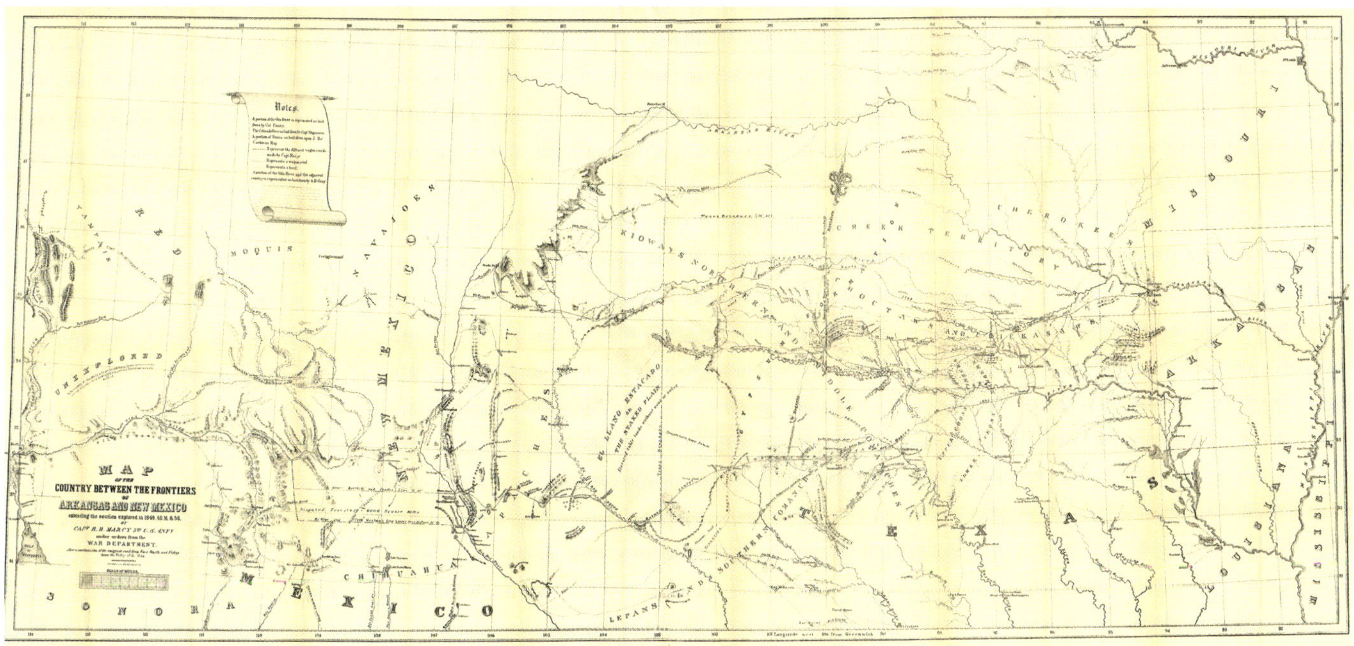

49

JAMES H. SIMPSON (1813–1883) · *MAP OF THE ROUTE PURSUED IN 1849 BY THE U. S. TROOPS, UNDER THE COMMAND OF BVT. LIEUT. COL. JNO. M. WASHINGTON, GOVERNOR OF NEW MEXICO, IN AN EXPEDITION AGAINST THE NAVAJO INDIANS BY J. H. SIMPSON, 1ST LIEUT. T. ENG'RS, ASSISTED BY MR. EDW. M. KERN; CONSTRUCTED UNDER THE GENERAL ORDERS OF COL. J. J. ABERT, CHIEF, TOP'L ENG'RS*

Philadelphia: P. S. Duval's Steam Press, 1850. 22 x 16 in. From: Joseph E. Johnston, W. F. Smith, et al, *Reports of the Secretary of War, with Reconnaissances of Routes from San Antonio to El Paso, by Bvt. Lt. Col. J. E. Johnston. Also the Report of Capt. R. B. Marcy's Route from Fort Smith to Santa Fe; and the Report of Lieut. J. H. Simpson of an Expedition into the Navajo Country* . . . 31st Cong., 1st Sess., Senate Ex. Doc. 64, Serial 562, 1850 (Washington, DC: Union Office, 1850).

James H. Simpson was a topographical engineer who was assigned to survey portions of New Mexico and Arizona. In 1849, he accompanied Col. John Washington on a punitive expedition against the Navajo Indians. This map shows the route of that expedition. Interestingly, Simpson thought part of his route would be a good railroad route through that part of the country.

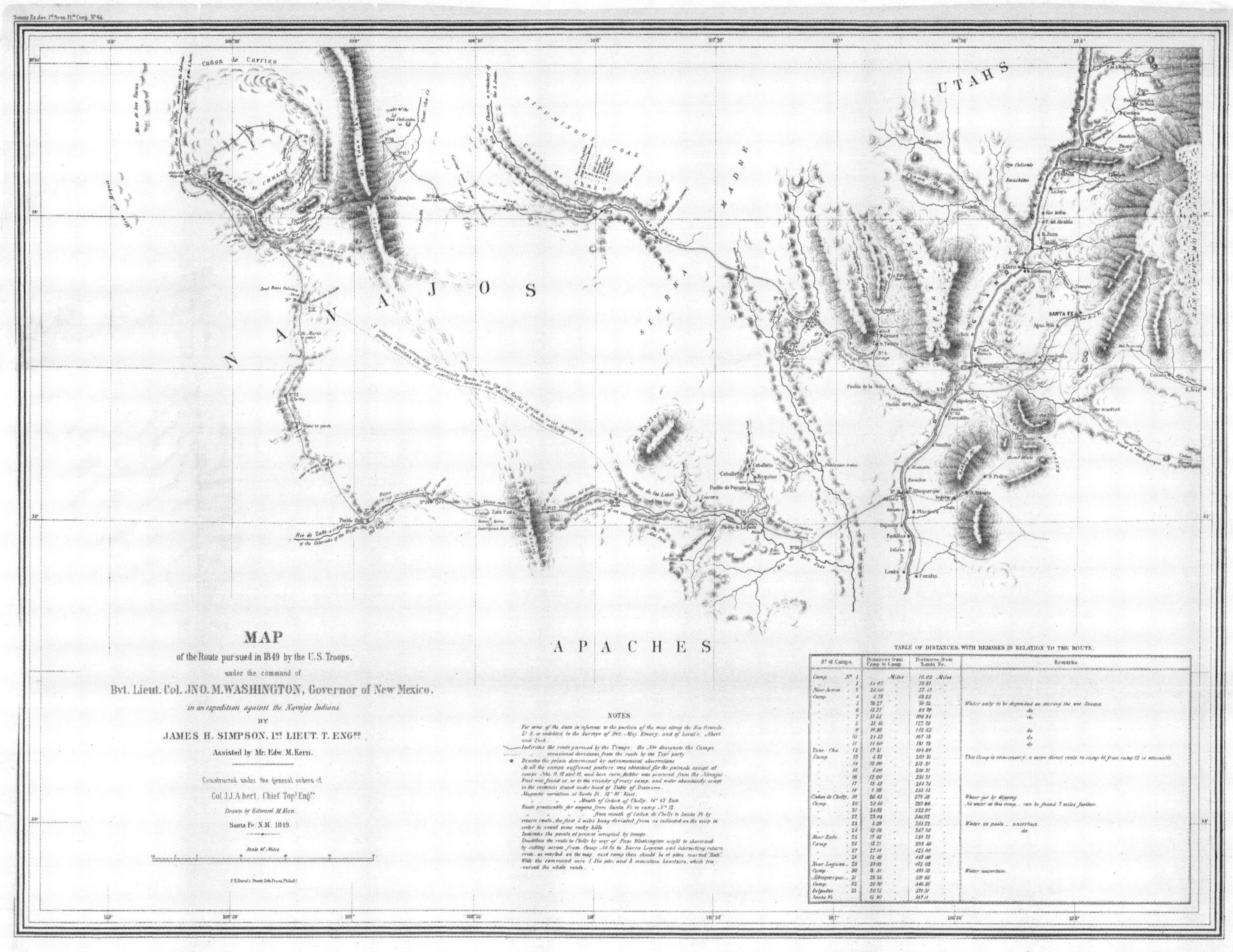
NAVAJOS
UTAHS
APACHES
SIERRA MADRE
SANTA FE
MAP
of the Route pursued in 1849 by the U.S. Troops,
under the command of
Bvt. Lieut. Col. JNO. M. WASHINGTON, Governor of New Mexico,
in an expedition against the Navajos Indians
BY
JAMES H. SIMPSON, 1st LIEUT. T. ENGRS
Assisted by Mr. Edw. M. Kern.
Constructed under the general orders of
Col. J.J. Abert, Chief Topl Engr.
Drawn by Edward M. Kern.
Santa Fe, N.M. 1849.
Scale of Miles
NOTES
TABLE OF DISTANCES, WITH REMARKS IN RELATION TO THE ROUTE.
No of Camps.
Distances from Camp to Camp.
Distances from Santa Fe.
Remarks
Water only to be depended on during the wet Season
This Camp is unnecessary; a more direct route to camp 14 from camp 12 is attainable
Water got by digging
No water at this camp... can be found 7 miles further
Water in pools ... uncertain.
Water uncertain.

50

RICHARD KERN (1821–1853) · *INDIAN WEAVING (PUEBLO ZUÑI)*

New York: Ackerman Lith., 1853. Lithograph, 7 x 4½ in. From: Lorenzo Sitgreaves: *Report of an Expedition Down the Zuñi and Colorado Rivers*, 32nd Cong., 2nd Sess., Senate Exec. Doc. 59, Serial 668 (Washington, DC: Robert Armstrong, 1853).

Lorenzo Sitgreaves was a topographical engineer who fought in the Mexican War under Gen. John Wool. During that time, he mapped the area from San Antonio, Texas through the Mexican province of Chihuahua. In 1851, following on James H. Simpson's recommendations, he led an expedition down the Zuni River to the Colorado River, looking for a possible railroad route. He felt the route he explored was too rugged and dangerous for use by a railroad, but within a few decades, the Santa Fe Railroad ran along the course he had explored and mapped. He was fascinated by Native American culture, and many of the illustrations in his report show a variety of their activities.

51

RICHARD KERN (1821–1853) · *BUFFALO DANCE, PUEBLO DE ZUÑI N.M.*

New York: Ackerman Lith.,1853. Lithograph, 7½ x 10 in. From: *Report of an Exploration Down the Zuñi and Colorado Rivers; Plate 1*, 32nd Cong., 2nd Sess., Senate Ex. Doc. 59 (Washington, DC: Robert Armstrong, 1853).

Despite the fact that Sitgreaves felt the route he explored was not suitable for a railroad—in part because of hostile Native Americans—many lithographs in his report are devoted to them. Richard Kern was a cartographer and artist on the Sitgreaves expedition who sketched many Native American scenes. He was killed by Ute Indians in 1853, while on one of the Pacific Railroad surveys.

52

HOWARD STANSBURY (1806–1863) · [Detail from:] *MAP OF A RECONNOISSANCE BETWEEN FORT LEAVENWORTH ON THE MISSOURI RIVER AND THE GREAT SALT LAKE IN THE TERRITORY OF UTAH, MADE IN 1849 AND 1850, . . . BY CAPT. HOWARD STANSBURY, . . .*

Assisted by Lt. J. W. Gunnison and Albert Carrington, Drawn by Lt. Gunnison and Charles Preuss. New York: Ackerman Lith., 1852. 68 x 28½ in. From: *An Expedition to the Valley of the Great Salt Lake of Utah: Including . . . A Reconnoissance of a New Route Through the Rocky Mountains, and Two Large and Accurate Maps of that Region*, 32nd Cong., Special Session, Senate Ex. Doc. 3, Serial 608 (Philadelphia: Lippincott, Grambo & Co. 1852).

In 1849, topographical engineer Capt. Howard Stansbury was sent from Fort Leavenworth to explore and map the Salt Lake Valley of Utah. Stansbury was to evaluate the emigrant trails that ran through Utah and look for possible railroad routes west. On the way to Utah, Stansbury's expedition mapped parts of the Oregon Trail and the Mormon Trail.

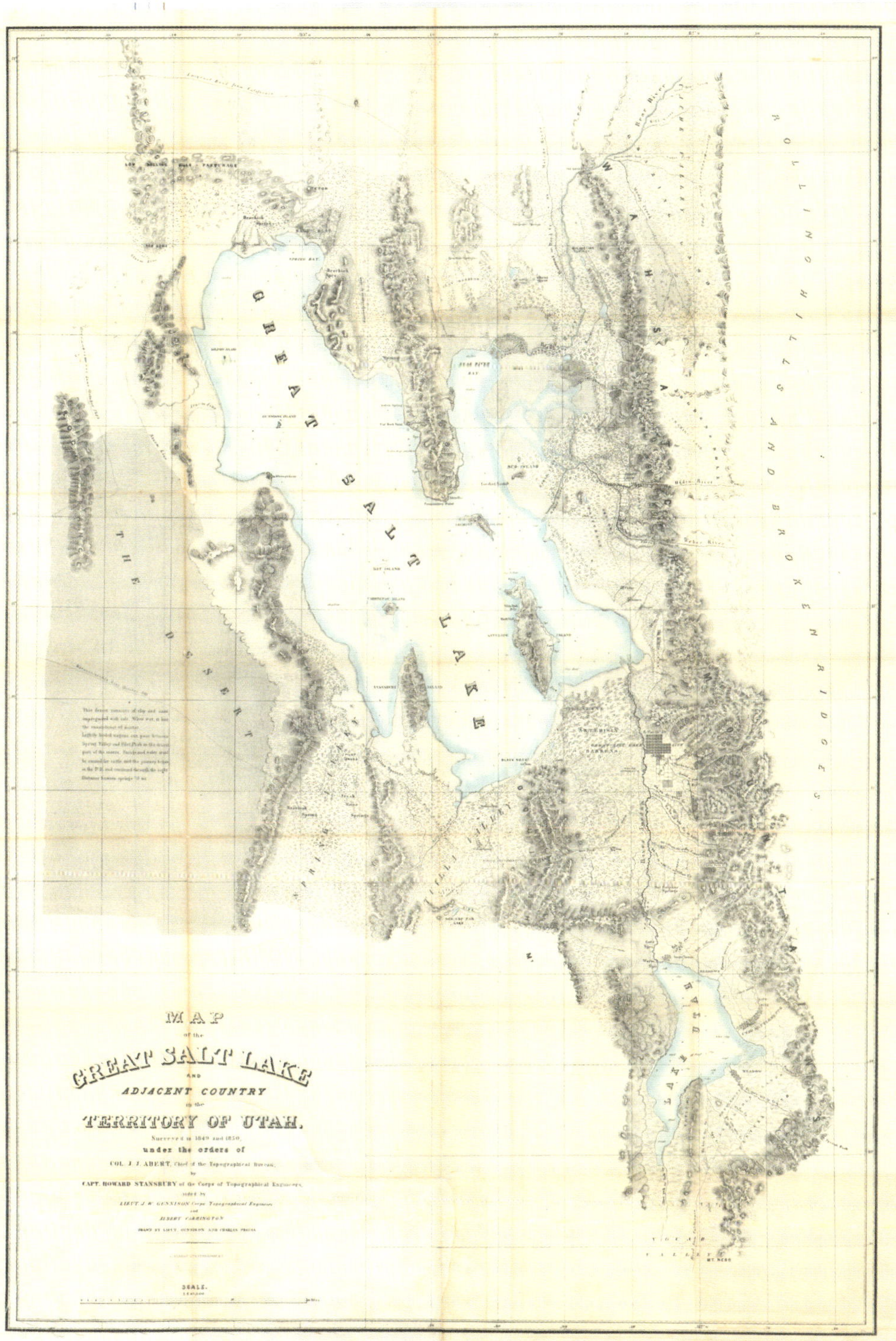
GREAT SALT LAKE
THE DESERT
ROLLING HILLS AND BROKEN RIDGES
UTAH LAKE
MAP
of the
GREAT SALT LAKE
AND
ADJACENT COUNTRY
in the
TERRITORY OF UTAH.
Surveyed in 1849 and 1850,
under the orders of
COL. J. J. ABERT, Chief of the Topographical Bureau,
by
CAPT. HOWARD STANSBURY of the Corps of Topographical Engineers,
SCALE.

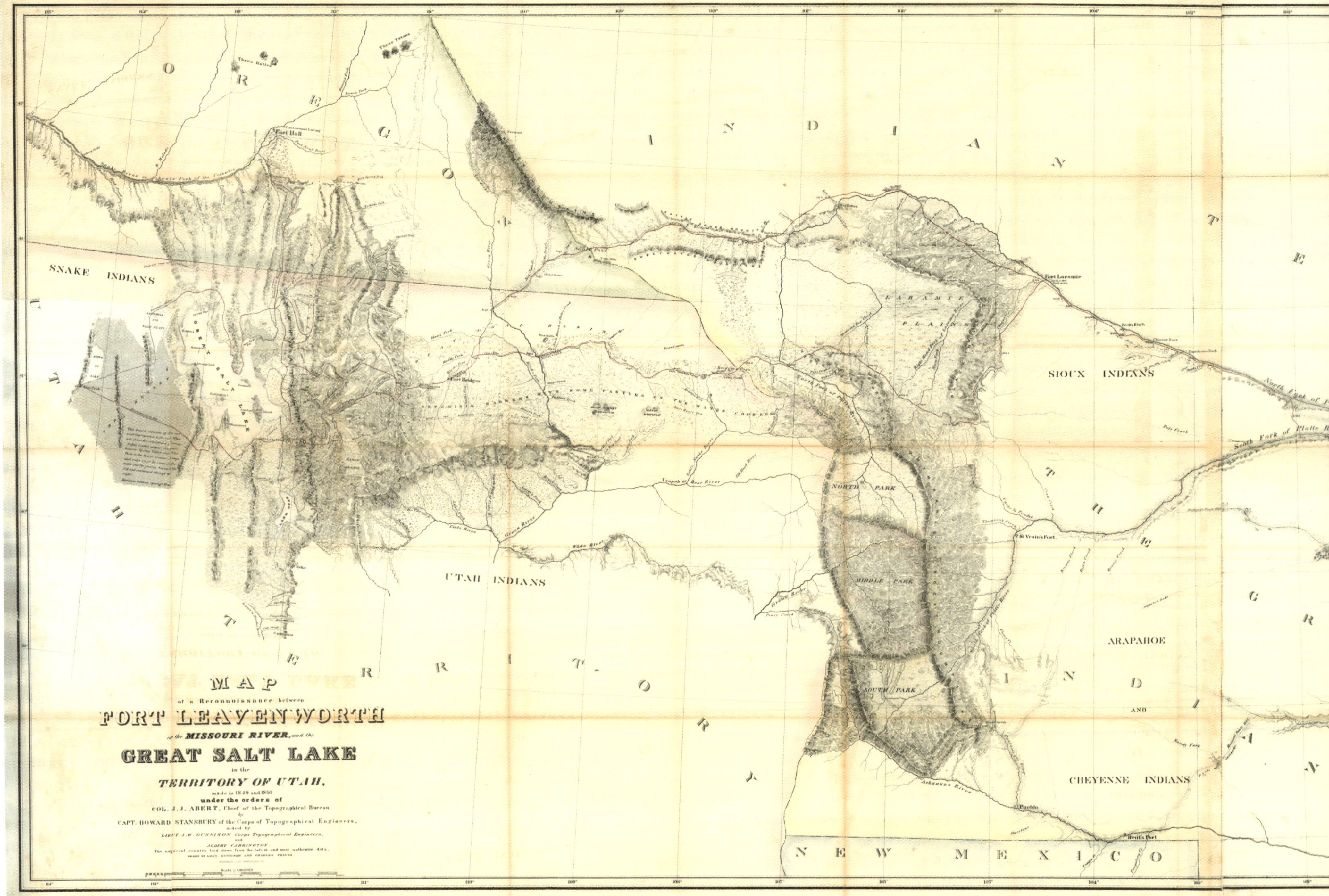

MAP
of a Reconnoissance between
FORT LEAVENWORTH
at the MISSOURI RIVER, and the
GREAT SALT LAKE
in the
TERRITORY OF UTAH,
made in 1849 and 1850
under the orders of
COL. J. J. ABERT, Chief of the Topographical Bureau,
by
CAPT. HOWARD STANSBURY of the Corps of Topographical Engineers,
aided by
LIEUT. J. W. GUNNISON Corps Topographical Engineers,
and
ALBERT CARRINGTON.
The adjacent country laid down from the latest and most authentic data.
DRAWN BY LIEUT. GUNNISON AND CHARLES PREUSS
O R E G O N
SNAKE INDIANS
U T A H T E R R I T O R Y
I N D I A N T E R R I T O R Y
Three Tetons
Three Buttes
Fort Hall
Fort Bridger
Fort Laramie
Scotts Bluffs
SIOUX INDIANS
North Fork of Platte
South Fork of Platte River
UTAH INDIANS
White River
Green River
Bear River
NORTH PARK
MIDDLE PARK
SOUTH PARK
St Vrain's Fort
ARAPAHOE AND CHEYENNE INDIANS
Arkansas River
Pueblo
Bent's Fort
N E W M E X I C O

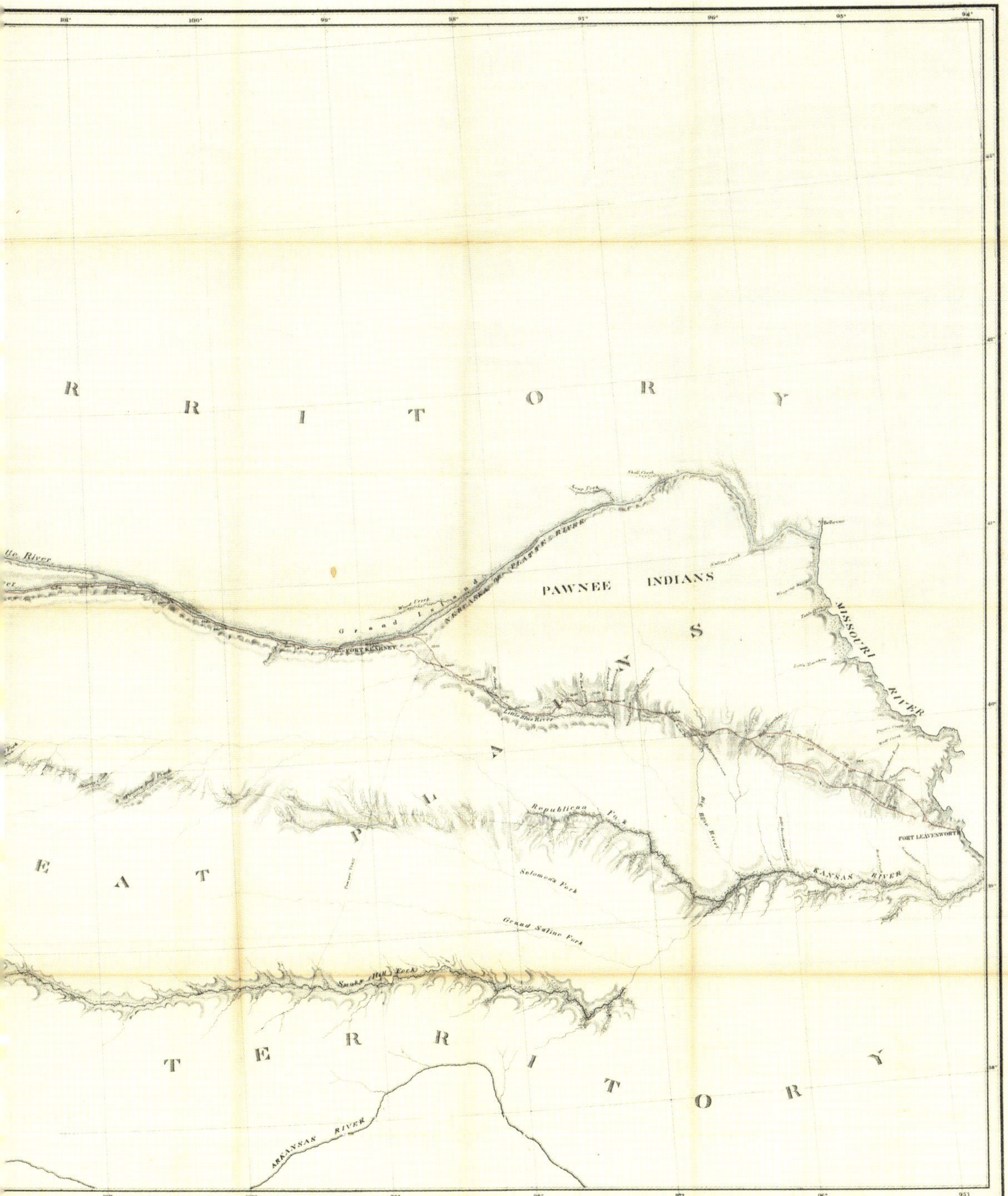

R R I T O R Y
PAWNEE INDIANS
MISSOURI RIVER
FORT LEAVENWORTH
KANSAN RIVER
Republican Fork
Solomon's Fork
Grand Saline Fork
Smoky Hill Fork
Big Blue River
E A T
T E R R I T O R Y
ARKANSAS RIVER

53

HOWARD STANSBURY (1806–1863)
MAP OF THE GREAT SALT LAKE AND ADJACENT COUNTRY IN THE TERRITORY OF UTAH . . .

Assisted by Lt. J. W. Gunnison and Albert Carrington, drawn by Lt. Gunnison and Charles Preuss. New York: Ackerman Lith., 1852. 30 x 43¼ in. From: *An Expedition to the Valley of the Great Salt Lake of Utah: Including . . . A Reconnoissance of a New Route Through the Rocky Mountains, and Two Large and Accurate Maps of that Region*, 32nd Cong., Special Session, Senate Ex. Doc. 3, Serial 608 (Philadelphia: Lippincott, Grambo & Co. 1852).

When Stansbury's expedition arrived in the Salt Lake Valley, the Mormons, who had recently settled the area, were highly suspicious of the expedition. However, Stansbury mollified them, and Brigham Young's secretary, Albert Carrington, was assigned to assist the group. Stansbury and his expedition spent the better part of two years exploring the Salt Lake area, devoting much time to identifying the plants and animals indigenous to Utah. This map illustrates the detailed geographical and topographical data that were gathered.

54

STREET IN GREAT SALT LAKE CITY-LOOKING EAST

New York: Ackerman Lith., 1852. Lithograph, 7¾ x 4½ in. From: Howard Stansbury: *An Expedition to the Valley of the Great Salt Lake of Utah: Including . . . A Reconnoissance of a New Route Through the Rocky Mountains, and Two Large and Accurate Maps of that Region,* 32nd Cong., Special Session, Senate Ex. Doc. 3, Serial 608 (Philadelphia: Lippincott, Grambo & Co. 1852).

John W. Gunnison, Stansbury's second-in-command, wrote a complimentary history of the Mormons that was a part of Stansbury's final report, and several illustrations in the report show life in Salt Lake City.

VI

FINDING THE BEST ROUTE: THE PACIFIC RAILROAD SURVEYS

Though there were some genuine geographical arguments for and against each of the railroad routes proposed in the 1840s and early 1850s, in the final analysis, one of the main issues was how its location might impact the expansion of slavery. As a result, unable to agree on a route for the railroad, and after much debate, Congress passed what became Section 10 of the Army Appropriation Act of 1853. That short section authorized the secretary of war to "make such explorations and surveys as be deemed advisable, to ascertain the most practicable and economical route for a railroad from the Mississippi River to the Pacific Ocean."[12] The secretary of war, pursuant to that statute, authorized five expeditions, four from various points near the Mississippi River to the Pacific Ocean, to determine which of the proposed routes would be the "most practicable and economical" for a Pacific Railroad, and one that would explore California and Oregon. There was a northern, north-central, south-central and a southern route. The product of these surveys, *Reports of Explorations and Surveys to Ascertain the Most Practicable and Economical Route for a Railroad from the Mississippi River to the Pacific Ocean, Made under the Direction of the Secretary of War, in 1853-4,* was a multi-volume set of reports on all sorts of subjects, including cartography, topography, geology, zoology, botany and ethnology. Indeed, it was the most comprehensive treatise on the West published in the nineteenth century.

The northern route expedition, which ran between the 47th and 49th parallels of north latitude, was headed by Isaac I. Stevens, the newly appointed governor of the Washington Territory. It began in St. Paul, Minnesota and ended at Puget Sound. Among those on that survey was George McClellan, who was to later become a general during the Civil War and Democratic candidate for president in 1864.

There was also a group that explored an area between the 38th and 39th parallels (and, later, the 41st parallel). The original head of that expedition was Capt. John Gunnison, who was killed by hostile Native Americans halfway through his trek, in modern-day Utah. The expedition was taken over by Lt. E. G. Beckwith, who became known as the "Explorer of the Central Rockies." South of the Central Rockies, an expedition traversed a 35th parallel route. The leader of that group was Capt. Amiel Weeks Whipple, a West Point graduate who also became a general in the Civil

12. *Public Laws Passed . . . at the Second Session of the Thirty Second Congress*, 219.

War. The southernmost route ran along the 32nd parallel. Two men explored this route: Capt. John G. Parke and Capt. John Pope (also to become a Civil War general). Though there was a lot of desert along the 32nd parallel route, the advantage was that there were no substantial mountains.

At the conclusion of the surveys, the preferred route of the secretary of war, Jefferson Davis from Mississippi, was the southern route, along the 32nd parallel. However, his preferred route was not adopted because many felt that would have made the export of slavery to the territories that much easier. Interestingly, the route that the Union Pacific and Central Pacific Railroads actually followed to complete the first transcontinental railroad was not surveyed, except in parts, by any of the four groups sent out in 1853 and 1854.

THE 47TH AND 49TH PARALLEL ROUTE

The northern route was to go west out of St. Paul in the Minnesota Territory, intersect the Missouri River, follow the Missouri to its headwaters, cross the Rocky Mountains in today's western Montana and eastern Idaho, and end up at Puget Sound, in Washington. Though almost fifty years had passed since Lewis and Clark's expedition, Governor Stevens's party was one of the few that had traversed that part of the country since Lewis and Clark. Therefore, Stevens and his expedition utilized the notes and maps of Lewis and Clark. Stevens's party included a naturalist, Dr. George Suckley; a surgeon; a linguist who was also an artist, Gustavus Sohon; and John Mix Stanley, an artist of the American West.

The expedition ultimately identified five passes across the northern Rockies and recommended two of them as possible railroad passes. The route through the Rockies was often very difficult. Two lithographs from the *Railroad Survey Reports* illustrate some of the terrain: Cantonment Stevens was one of the mountain camps for Stevens's party (fig. 55); the Hell Gate was a treacherous river crossing (fig. 59). Despite the rugged terrain, the Stevens party found several passes through the Rockies that were suitable for a railroad (fig. 56).

Crossing the Cascade Mountains was more of a challenge. Initially, Capt. George McClellan, beginning at Puget Sound, was given the task of locating a satisfactory pass or passes through the Cascades. However, he refused to go into one pass during the snowy season to see if it was suitable for a railroad in the winter. He also failed to examine other, better, passes. The Washington Territorial Legislature ultimately had to field another party, headed by Frederick W. Lander, a civil engineer, to locate satisfactory passes through the Cascades.

THE 38TH, 39TH AND 41ST PARALLEL ROUTES

The 38th and 39th parallel route was championed by Missouri senator Thomas Hart Benton. It would pass through his state, and provided an essentially straight shot to the Pacific. (St. Louis, in the east, is on the 39th parallel of north latitude and San Francisco is on the 38th parallel.) Capt.

Gunnison headed the expedition and was accompanied by Richard Kern, a topographer and artist and by Frederick Creuzefeldt, a German botanist. Gunnison's assistant was Lt. E. G. Beckwith. The proposed route was to go up the Kansas River to the Arkansas River; up the Arkansas to the base of the Rockies; over the Sangre de Cristo Pass, southwest of present-day Pueblo, Colorado; across and out of the San Luis Valley of what is now Colorado; and through present-day Utah, Nevada and into California.

All went relatively well until the party entered the territory claimed by the Ute Indians, who harassed the party through the Wasatch Mountains and as it traveled westward. Near Sevier Lake, southwest of the Great Salt Lake, on October 26, 1853, Gunnison and a part of the party were ambushed by a band of Utes, and he, Kern, Creuzefeldt and several others were killed. Lieutenant Beckwith, who was elsewhere with another part of the party at the time, returned to Great Salt Lake City and spent the winter there. Lieutenant Beckwith prepared the map illustrated here, but near Sevier Lake, in the lower right-hand corner of the map, he marked the spot where Gunnison and his party were killed (fig. 57). Several other cartographers also identified the location of Gunnison's death.

In early 1854, Beckwith, along with Prussian topographer and artist Baron F. W. von Egloffstein, James Schiel, a German geologist, and others, backtracked a bit, to Fort Bridger, which was northeast of Salt Lake City and across the Wasatch Mountains, at about the 41st parallel of north latitude. During that trek, Beckwith identified Utah's Weber River and the Timpanogos Canyon as satisfactory for a railroad. The party then returned to Salt Lake City and went north again, back to the 41st parallel of north latitude. It then went across the Great Basin to the Humboldt River, and from the Humboldt to the base of the Sierra Nevada Mountains (fig. 58). The party then located two suitable passes through the Sierra Nevada Mountains, to the Sacramento River Valley in California, and ended the trip.

THE 35TH PARALLEL ROUTE

Lieutenant Amiel Weeks Whipple, the leader of the 35th parallel survey, had worked for the both US Coast Survey and the US-Mexico Boundary Survey Commission. His party included Dr. Jules Marcou, a Swiss geologist and Heinrich Balduin Möllhausen, a Prussian geographer and artist. The expedition began not far from Fort Smith, Arkansas (fig. 60). It then went up the Canadian River, to one of its sources. From there, the party traveled to Anton Chico, on the Pecos River, and from there, to Albuquerque, New Mexico, then west through Zuñi and Hopi Indian country, to the Colorado River south of a geologic formation known as "The Needles." The expedition then crossed the Mojave Desert, went through California's Cajon Pass and ended in San Bernardino. Although all of the Pacific Railroad survey parties were directed to record and report on the cultures of the various Native American tribes on their routes, Whipple perhaps took this admonition the most seriously. His report is filled with this information, and includes many illustrations of tribal members, cultural activities and history (fig. 61).

THE 32ND PARALLEL ROUTE

Much of the route along the 32nd parallel had previously been explored during the Mexican War by Lt. Col. W. H. Emory and later by a civilian surveyor, A. B. Gray, for the Texas Western Rail Road Company. However, two portions of the 32nd parallel route were explored as a part of the Pacific Railroad surveys. Lt. John G. Parke traveled from current-day central Arizona (not far from Phoenix) to the Rio Grande River. He concluded that there were only nine locations with a permanent water supply and recommended drilling artesian wells along the route. Another portion of the 32nd parallel route was explored by Capt. John Pope. He went from Doña Ana, on the Rio Grande, north of Franklin, Texas (now El Paso) to Preston, on the Red River. Lieutenant Parke's map traced a route through the very new Gadsden Purchase and Captain Pope's map is one of the first to show Dallas, Texas (fig. 62).

THE CALIFORNIA, OREGON, AND WASHINGTON SURVEYS

Lt. R. S. Williamson was in charge of this part of the exploration, assisted by Lt. H. L. Abbott and Lt. John G. Parke (before he went to explore the 32nd parallel route). German cartographer Charles Preuss, who had been on several of John C. Fremont's expeditions, was attached to the expedition, as well as Thomas Antisell, a Scottish geologist. There were primarily two objectives in the west coast surveys: to identify suitable railroad passes through the Sierra Nevada Mountains and the California Coast Range (fig. 63) and to determine a route that would connect California with Oregon and Washington.

55

GUSTAVUS SOHON (1825–1903) · *CANTONMENT STEVENS, LOOKING WESTWARD*

New York: Sarony, Major & Knapp, 1860. Lithograph, 6½ x 9½ in. From: *Reports of Explorations and Surveys, to Ascertain the Most Practicable and Economical Route for a Railroad from the Mississippi River to the Pacific Ocean, Made Under the Direction of the Secretary of War, in 1853–4; Plate LIX*, 36th Cong., 1st Sess., Senate Ex. Doc. [Unnumbered], Vol. XII, Book I (Washington, DC: Thomas H. Ford, 1860).

Gustavus Sohon was a Prussian who immigrated to the US to avoid service in the Prussian Army, but then joined the US Army. He was assigned to Gov. Isaac I. Stevens's expedition, and his drawings were used to illustrate Stevens's portion of the *Pacific Railroad Reports*. This detailed image of Cantonment Stevens, one of the expedition's encampments named after the leader of the survey, is one of ten Sohon illustrations in the *Pacific Railroad Reports*.

CANTONMENT STEVENS, LOOKING WESTWARD

Lake Pend Oreille
Camp Campbell
CLARK'S FORK
Route of Lieut. R. Saxton in July & Aug. 1853
Route of Lieut. Donelson & Main Train in October 1853
Hot Spring
Prairie Hills
Hot Spring Creek
Flathead Lake
Swan River
Flathead River
High rugged mountains and pine forest unexplored
Route of A. W. Tinkham in September 1853
Trading Post
Mountains and timber
Womans Breast
Gravel Bottom Fork
Route of J. Doty in June
Route of F. W. Lander
Breast R. or Teton
Route of J. Doty in May
Nah too-see
Medicine or Sun River
Route of Gov. Stevens, Lt. Donelson & Main T
Lewis & Clark's Pass
Cadott's Pass
THE ROCKY MOUNTAINS
Mountains with pine forest unexplored
Coeur d' Alêne River
Stevens Peak
Route of Gov. Stevens & J. M. Stanley in October 1853
Regis Borgia Cr.
Horse Plain
F. W. Lander
Mountains with pine forest
Bitter Root River
Bitter Root Mountains
Approximate divide between
Defile of Coriacan
Blackfoot Fork
Route of Lieut. Donelson & Main Train in September
Mountains and pine forest
Hell Gate River
Route of Lieut. Mullan in Sept. 1853 & March 1854
Little Blackfoot River
Hell Gate Passes
Lou Lou Fork
Fort Owen
Camp Bache Sep. 29 to Oct. 3
Cantonment Stevens
Tinkham in November 1853
Hot Spr. Jan. 1. 1854
Deer Lodge Prairie
Mountains & timber
Route of Lieut. Mullan in September 1854
Salmon Fork
Koos koos ky River
Lewis and Clark's

56

ISAAC I. STEVENS

[Detail from:] *MAP NO. 3, ROCKY MOUNTAINS TO PUGET SOUND, ROUTE NEAR THE 47TH AND 49TH PARALLELS*

37 x 25 in. From: *Reports of Explorations and Surveys to Ascertain the Most Practicable and Economical Route for a Railroad from the Mississippi River to the Pacific Ocean, Made Under the Direction of the Secretary of War, in 1853–4*, 33rd Cong., 2nd Sess., Senate Ex. Doc. No. 78, Serial 768, Vol. XI (Washington, DC: Beverly Tucker, 1857).

This is a portion of one of the three major maps produced by the Pacific Railroad Survey headed by Isaac Stevens. Stevens went from St. Paul, Minnesota, between the 47th and 49th parallels of north latitude, to the Puget Sound. This detail shows several of the possible railroad routes through the Rocky Mountains.

57

E. G. BECKWITH (1818–1881)

[Detail from:] *MAP NO. 2 FROM GREAT SALT LAKE TO THE HUMBOLDT MOUNTAINS, ROUTE NEAR THE 41ST PARALLEL*

18¼ x 21 in. From: *Reports of Explorations and Surveys to Ascertain the Most Practicable and Economical Route for a Railroad from the Mississippi River to the Pacific Ocean, Made Under the Direction of the Secretary of War, in 1853–4,* 33rd Cong., 2nd Sess., Senate Ex. Doc. No. 78, Serial 768, Vol. XI (Washington, DC: Beverly Tucker, 1857).

John W. Gunnison was designated to lead a Pacific Railroad survey from the Mississippi River, along the 38th parallel of north latitude (basically across present-day Colorado, Utah and Nevada), to San Francisco. However, Gunnison and some of his men were killed by Ute Indians near Sevier Lake, southwest of the Great Salt Lake. This map detail marks the location of Gunnison's death, because Lieutenant Beckwith, his second-in-command, wanted to insure that people did not forget where Captain Gunnison had lost his life.

FOR A RAILROAD
ROUTE BELIEVED TO BE PRACTICABLE
EXPLORED IN 1854
GRANITE
MOUNTAIN
Magn. Var. 15°30'
UTAH LAKE
40°00'
39°30'
39°00'
I N D I A N S
Sevier River
Capt. J.W. Gunnison killed by Indians
Parvant Butte
SEVIER LAKE
Y

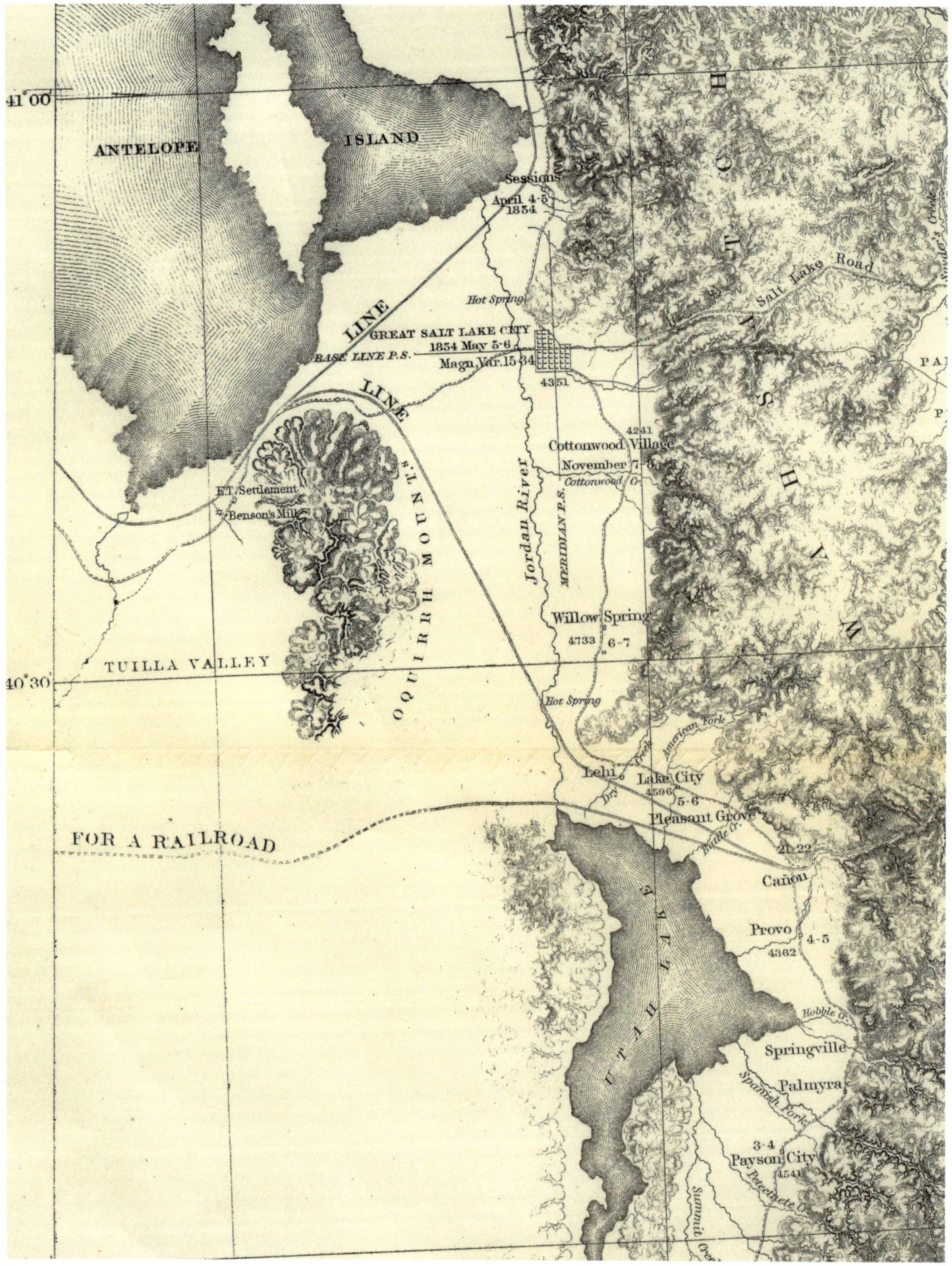

ANTELOPE
ISLAND
Sessions
April 4-5
1854
Hot Spring
LINE
GREAT SALT LAKE CITY
1854 May 5-6
BASE LINE P.S.
Magn. Var. 15 34
4351
LINE
Salt Lake Road
Cottonwood Village
November 7-8
Cottonwood Cr.
E.T. Settlement
Benson's Mill
OQUIRRH MOUNTS.
Jordan River
MERIDIAN P.S.
Willow Spring
4733
6-7
TUILLA VALLEY
41°00
40°30
Hot Spring
American Fork
Lehi
Lake City
4596
5-6
Pleasant Grove
FOR A RAILROAD
21-22
Cañon
Provo
4362
4-5
UTAH LAKE
Hobble Cr.
Springville
Palmyra
Spanish Fork
3-4
Payson City
4541
Summit Creek

58

E. G. BECKWITH (1818–1881)

[Detail from:] *MAP NO. 1 FROM THE VALLEY OF GREEN RIVER TO THE GREAT SALT LAKE, ROUTE NEAR THE 41ST PARALLEL*

18 x 20¾ in. From: *Reports of Explorations and Surveys to Ascertain the Most Practicable and Economical Route for a Railroad from the Mississippi River to the Pacific Ocean, Made Under the Direction of the Secretary of War, in 1853–4*, 33rd Cong., 2nd Sess., Senate Ex. Doc. No. 78, Serial 768, Vol. XI (Washington, DC: Beverly Tucker, 1857).

After Capt. John Gunnison's death, Lieutenant Beckwith was assigned to complete the portion of the Pacific Railroad survey Gunnison and he had begun. After wintering in Salt Lake City, Beckwith went north, instead of south, and traced a route along the 41st parallel of north latitude. This track ran through present-day Wyoming, instead of Gunnison's earlier route, through present-day Colorado. As it turned out, the Beckwith route was easier than Gunnison's, and some of it was used by the Union Pacific Railroad, in the first transcontinental crossing.

59

GUSTAVUS SOHON (1825–1905) · *CROSSING THE HELLGATE RIVER, MAY 5TH 1854*

New York: Sarony, Major & Knapp, 1860. Lithograph, 6½ x 9½ in. From: *Reports of Explorations and Surveys to Ascertain the Most Practicable and Economical Route for a Railroad from the Mississippi River to the Pacific Ocean, Made Under the Direction of the Secretary of War, in 1853–4; Plate LVI*, 36th Cong., 1st Sess., Senate Ex. Doc. [Unnumbered], Vol. XII, Book I (Washington, DC: Thomas Ford, 1860).

This Sohon illustration is one of very few that shows members of the expedition actually engaged in work activities. It is thought that one of the people shown in this lithograph is Sohon himself.

CROSSING THE HELLGATE RIVER MAY 5TH 1854.

⇝ 60 ⇜

H. B. MÖLLHAUSEN (1825–1905) · *FORT SMITH, ARKANSAS*

Philadelphia: T. Sinclair's Lith. 1854. Lithograph, 6½ x 9½ in. From: *Reports of Explorations and Surveys to Ascertain the Most Practicable and Economical Route for a Railroad from the Mississippi River to the Pacific Ocean, Made Under the Direction of the Secretary of War, in 1853–4,* 33rd Cong., 2nd Sess., Senate Ex. Doc. No. 78, Vol. III (Washington DC: Beverly Tucker, 1856).

Lt. Amiel Weeks Whipple headed up the Pacific Railroad survey that went west along the 35th parallel of north latitude. H. Balduin Möllhausen was a German national who, at the suggestion of Alexander de Humboldt, came to the United States and joined the railroad survey headed by Lieutenant Whipple. Möllhausen was an accomplished artist, and a number of his lithographs, like this one, illustrate landmarks of the country through which Whipple and his expedition traveled.

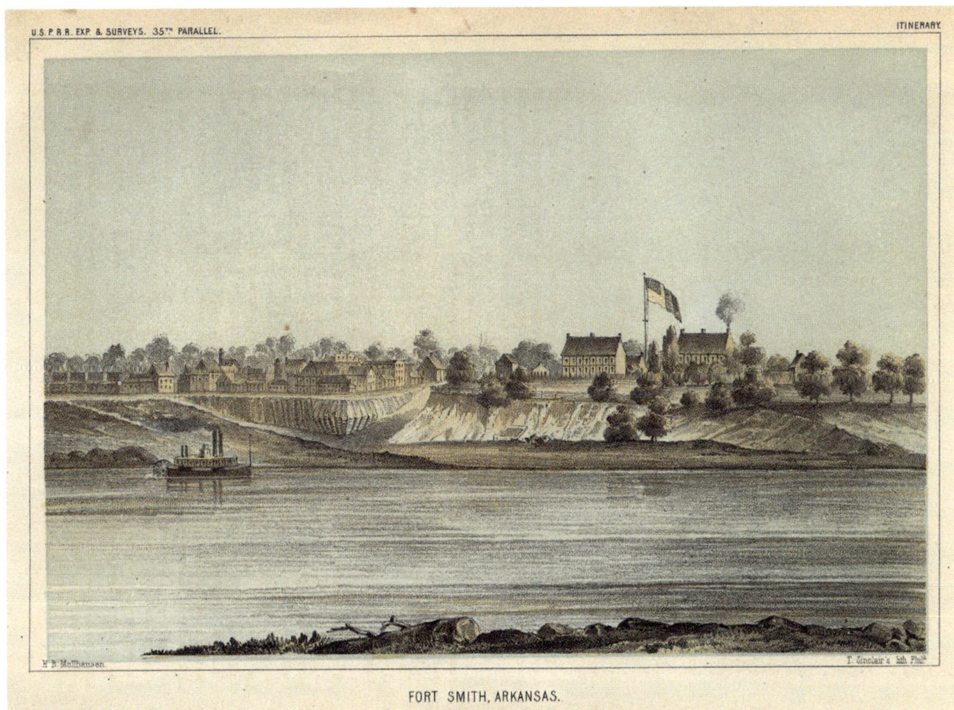

61

H. B. MÖLLHAUSEN (1825–1905) · *NAVAJOS*

Philadelphia: T. Sinclair's Lith. 1855. Lithograph, 6½ x 9½ in. From: *Reports of Explorations and Surveys to Ascertain the Most Practicable and Economical Route for a Railroad from the Mississippi River to the Pacific Ocean, Made Under the Direction of the Secretary of War, in 1853–4*, 33rd Cong., 2nd Sess., Senate Ex. Doc. No. 78, Vol. III (Washington DC: Beverly Tucker, 1856).

Möllhausen was very interested in Native Americans and their culture, and a number of his lithographs showed them in traditional costumes and engaging in tribal rituals. After he returned to Germany, Möllhausen became quite famous by writing stories about the American West.

U.S. P. R.R. EXP. & SURVEYS. 35TH PARALLEL.
INDIAN REPORT.
H. B. Möllhausen.
T. Sinclair's lith, Phil^a.

NAVAJOS.

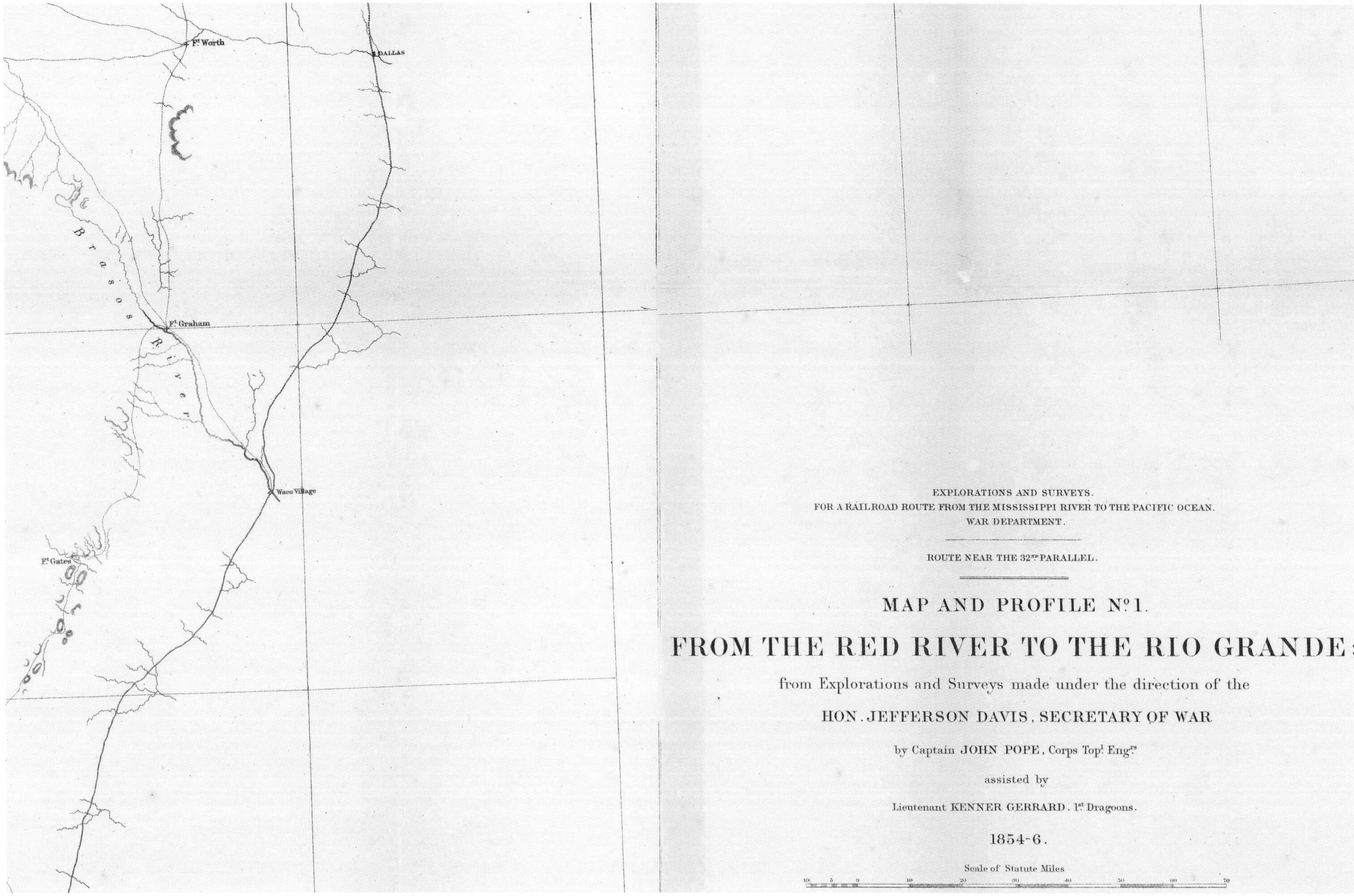
Ft. Worth
DALLAS
Brasos River
Ft. Graham
Waco Village
Ft. Gates
EXPLORATIONS AND SURVEYS.
FOR A RAILROAD ROUTE FROM THE MISSISSIPPI RIVER TO THE PACIFIC OCEAN.
WAR DEPARTMENT.
ROUTE NEAR THE 32ND PARALLEL.
MAP AND PROFILE No. 1.
FROM THE RED RIVER TO THE RIO GRANDE;
from Explorations and Surveys made under the direction of the
HON. JEFFERSON DAVIS, SECRETARY OF WAR
by Captain JOHN POPE, Corps Topl. Engrs.
assisted by
Lieutenant KENNER GERRARD. 1st. Dragoons.
1854-6.
Scale of Statute Miles
10 5 0 10 20 30 40 50 60 70

62

JOHN POPE (1822–1892)

[Detail from:] *MAP AND PROFILE NO. 1 FROM THE RED RIVER TO THE RIO GRANDE, ROUTE NEAR THE 32ND PARALLEL*

57½ x 27¾ in. From: *Reports of Explorations and Surveys to Ascertain the Most Practicable and Economical Route for a Railroad from the Mississippi River to the Pacific Ocean, Made Under the Direction of the Secretary of War, in 1853–4,* 33rd Cong., 2nd Sess., Senate Ex. Doc. No. 78, Vol. XI (Washington, DC: Beverly Tucker, 1857).

John Pope was a West Point graduate and a topographical engineer who, after the Mexican War, was assigned to survey part of a route along the 32nd parallel of north latitude for a possible transcontinental railroad. This map is one of the first to show the newly established town of Dallas, Texas.

63

ROBERT S. WILLIAMSON (1825–1882)

[Detail from:] *MAP OF PASSES IN THE SIERRA NEVADA, FROM WALKER'S PASS TO THE COAST RANGE*

Engraved By Selmer Siebert. 30½ x 19½ in. From: *Reports of Explorations and Surveys to Ascertain the Most Practicable and Economical Route for a Railroad From the Mississippi River to the Pacific Ocean, Made Under the Direction of the Secretary of War, in 1853–4*, 33rd Cong., 2nd Sess., Senate Ex. Doc. No. 78, Vol. XI (Washington, DC: Beverly Tucker, 1857).

Robert Williamson was a West Point graduate and a topographical engineer. During the Pacific Railroad surveys, he led a group whose main task was to survey passes in the Sierra Nevada Mountains of California that might be usable by railroads. His expedition also evaluated and mapped the West Coast, from Los Angeles to the Washington Territory, for possible railroad routes.

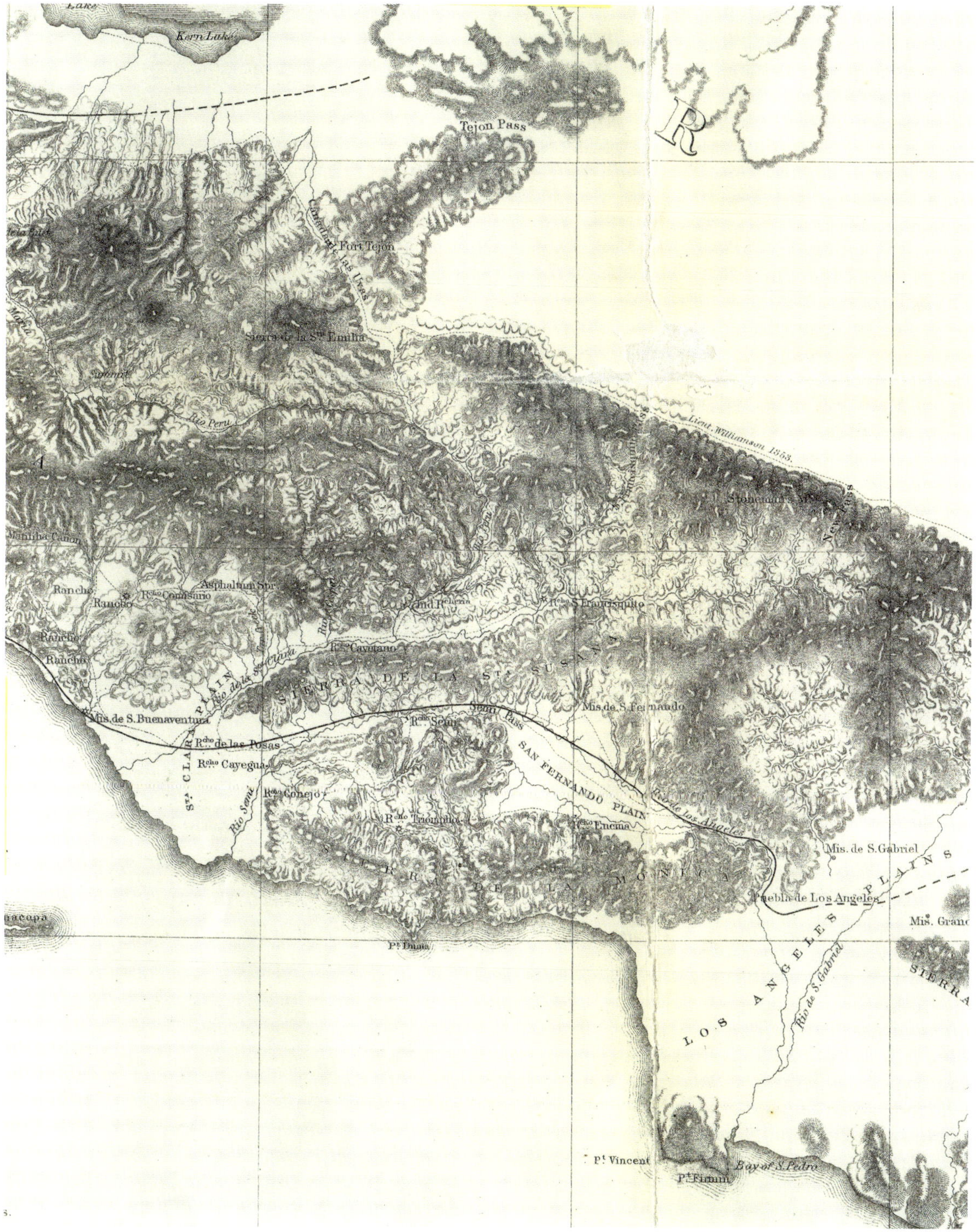
Kern Lake
Tejon Pass
R
Fort Tejon
Sierra de la Sta. Emilia
Rio Peru
Lieut. Williamson 1853.
Rancho
Asphaltum Spr.
Rcho. Comisario
Rcho. Cayetano
Rcho. S. Franciscuito
SIERRA DE LA Sta. SUSANA
Mis. de S. Fernando
Mis. de S. Buenaventura
Rcho. de las Posas
Rcho. Cayegua
Rcho. Conejo
Rcho. Simi
SAN FERNANDO PLAIN
Rio Simi
Rcho. Encina
Mis. de S. Gabriel
Puebla de Los Angeles
SIERRA DE LA MONICA
Pt. Duma
LOS ANGELES PLAINS
Rio de S. Gabriel
Pt. Vincent
Pt. Firmin
Bay of S. Pedro

VII

BUT WHAT ABOUT THE NATIVE AMERICANS?

ALTHOUGH THE STORY of what happened to the Native American population in North America after the Europeans arrived is a story that occupies shelves of books, any history of the westward expansion of the United States in the nineteenth century would be incomplete without some mention of the nation's relations with them. At the outset, three fundamental concepts should be mentioned. The first is that there was never a single entity known as "Native Americans" who shared common goals and ends. In fact, one of the most commonly used techniques of Europeans in dealings with Native Americans was "divide and conquer." Second, Europeans never accepted the concept that Native Americans "owned" the vast areas of the North American continent over which they roamed. Perhaps the most concise statement of that attitude was articulated in 1802, by John Quincy Adams, in a speech to descendants of some of the first European settlers:

> The Indian right of possession itself stands, with regard to the greatest part of the country, upon a questionable foundation. Their cultivated fields, their constructed habitations, a space of ample sufficiency for their subsistence, and whatever they had annexed to themselves, by personal labor, was undoubtedly by the laws of nature theirs. But what is the right of a huntsman of a forest of a thousand miles over which he has accidentally ranged in quest of prey? Shall the liberal bounties of providence to the race of man be monopolized by one of ten thousand for whom they were created? . . . Shall the lordly savage not only disdain the virtues and enjoyments of civilization himself, but shall he control the civilization of a world? Shall he forbid the wilderness to blossom like the rose?[13]

Adams's answer, and the answer of almost everyone else in nineteenth-century America was a resounding NO! Third, by the middle of the eighteenth century, the Native American population of North America was shrinking dramatically, due to disease, warfare and many other causes, and the European population was expanding rapidly. And although at the conclusion of the French and Indian War, in 1763, Great Britain attempted to set aside the area from the tops of the Allegheny Mountains to the Mississippi River for Native Americans (fig. 64), that effort was unsuccessful. In fact, by the end of the American Revolution, in the 1780s, when the American western boundary was set at the Mississippi River, vast tracts of land west of the Alleghenies were occupied by Europeans or claimed as land that could and should be settled by Revolutionary War veterans.

13. John Quincy Adams, "Speech to Sons of the Pilgrims, December 22, 1802," in *U. S. Department of the Interior, Report on Indian Affairs by the Acting Commissioner for the Year 1867* (Washington, DC: Government Printing Office, 1868), 144.

By the time Lewis and Clark started their journey west, the new United States government had negotiated a number of treaties with Native American tribes. In a few of them, the Americans and their counterparties were more or less equal negotiating partners, but the vast majority of these resulted from a defeat of the Native Americans by United States military forces. For example, the 1795 Treaty of Greenville was concluded after the Battle of Fallen Timbers, in which Gen. "Mad Anthony" Wayne defeated several tribes. That treaty basically opened Ohio to settlement. In his instructions to Meriwether Lewis, President Jefferson was quite clear regarding interactions with Native Americans:

> The commerce which may be carried on with the people inhabiting the line you will pursue, renders a knolege [*sic*] of these people important. You will therefore endeavor to make yourself acquainted . . . with the names of the nations & their numbers; the extent & limits of their possessions: their relations with other tribes or nations; . . . And considering the interest which every nation has in extending & strengthening the authority of reason & justice among the people around them, it will be useful to acquire what knolege [*sic*] you can of the state of morality, religion & information among them, as it may better enable those who endeavor to civilize & instruct them, to adapt their measures to the existing notions & practices of those on whom they are to operate.[14]

Jefferson also indicated in his instructions that Lewis should procure "light articles for barter, & presents among the Indians." Among those items were "peace medals," for presentation to certain of the tribal chiefs. That tradition was carried over into subsequent presidential administrations (fig. 65).

Whether Jefferson had it in his mind that Native Americans in the West would be left alone, or displaced as settlers moved west, or didn't have any opinion on the subject, it was less than a generation later that the die was cast regarding their fate. Although President Andrew Jackson is often thought to be the driving force behind the forceful re-settlement of Native Americans beyond the Mississippi River, that idea did not originate with him. Indeed, Native Americans began to be resettled west as early as 1817. In his Message to Congress on December 7, 1824, President James Monroe said:

> Experience has shown that unless the tribes be civilized they can never be incorporated into our system in any form whatever. It has likewise been shown that in the regular augmentation of our population with the extension of our settlements their situation will become deplorable . . . Between the limits of our present states and territories and the Rocky Mountains and Mexico there is a vast territory to which they might be invited with inducements which might be successful. It is thought if that territory should be divided into districts by previous agreement with the tribes now residing there and civil governments be established in each, with schools for every branch of instruction in literature and the arts of civilized life, that all the tribes now within our limits might gradually be drawn there.[15]

In 1836, Albert Gallatin, Thomas Jefferson's secretary of the treasury and a widely respected ethnologist of Native Americans, prepared a map for the American Antiquarian Society. It showed the distribution of many of the major Native American tribes, in the East as of 1600, and in the West as of 1800 (fig. 66). In 1834, Congress had defined "Indian Country" in the West as: "All that part of the United States west of the Mississippi, and not

---

14. www.presidency.ucsb.edu/ws/?pid=66430 (accessed July 30, 2017).
15. Ibid.

within the states of Missouri and Louisiana, or the territory of Arkansas."[16] By the time of Gallatin's map, with very few exceptions, Native Americans lived west of the Mississippi River, with eastern tribes ultimately being settled (as "emigrants") in a portion of "Indian Country" (fig. 67) and Plains Native Americans still ranging quite widely throughout the Great Plains and Inter-Mountain West.

Make no mistake about it. In the nineteenth century, to the extent Native Americans were perceived as standing in the way of American "progress," they were going to be swept away. In fact, though it was not created until 1872, a painting by John Gast called *American Progress* was emblematic of the attitude toward Native Americans throughout the nineteenth century. The painting was widely reproduced (fig. 68) and is dominated by a very large female figure floating across the landscape from the cities of the East toward the mountains of the West. In one hand, she holds a schoolbook, and in the other, a roll of telegraph wire, unspooling it as she progresses. Moving west, below her, are wagon trains, stagecoaches, railroads, farmers, miners and hunters. Fading into the western mountains are Native Americans, and buffalo and other wild game. This scene was Manifest Destiny, illustrated.

---

16. *An Act to Regulate Trade and Intercourse with the Indian Tribes, and to Preserve Peace on the Frontiers*. 23rd Cong. 1st Sess., Ch. 161, June 30, 1834.

64

J. GIBSON · *THE BRITISH GOVERNMENTS IN NTH. AMERICA LAID DOWN AGREEABLE TO THE PROCLAMATION OF OCT^{R} 7, 1763*

9½ x 7 in. From: *The Gentlemen's Magazine and Historical Chronicle,* Vol. XXXIII, for the Year M.DCC.LXIII (London: D. Henry and R. Cave, 1763).

Very little is known about J. Gibson, except that he drew several maps for London's *Gentleman's Magazine* in the 1760s. This map shows the so-called Proclamation Line, decreed by King George III in October 1763, at the conclusion of the French and Indian War. It purportedly ran along the highest points of the Allegheny Mountains. Its goal was to separate the British subjects from the Native Americans. It never worked. By the time the line was established, Americans had already crossed the Alleghenies and begun to encroach on land claimed by Native Americans.

65

PRESIDENT JAMES MADISON PEACE AND FRIENDSHIP MEDAL

2⅞ in. diam., bronze, [c. 1840s].

Peace medals as gifts for important Native American chiefs were first given by Lewis and Clark on their expedition to the Pacific in 1804–06. This commemorative version of the medal used during the James Madison administration features a profile of President Madison on the obverse, and two clasped hands, a peace pipe crossed with a hatchet, and the words "Peace and Friendship" on the reverse.

66

ALBERT GALLATIN (1761–1849) · *MAP OF THE INDIAN TRIBES OF NORTH AMERICA ABOUT 1600 A. D. ALONG THE ATLANTIC; & ABOUT 1800 A.D. WESTWARDLY*

Boston: Pendleton's Lithography, 1836. 16¾ x 15⅛ in. From: *Archaeologica Americana: Transactions and Collections of the American Antiquarian Society*, Vol. II (Cambridge, Mass.: Folsom, Wells & Thurston, 1836).

Albert Gallatin was a Swiss polymath who immigrated to the newly established United States in the 1780s. He entered politics and served in Congress, as secretary of the treasury under Jefferson and as ambassador to France and to Great Britain. Later in life, he helped found what is now New York University and the American Ethnological Society. This map reflected Gallatin's long-time interest in Native American history and culture.

"WESTWARD THE COURSE OF EMPIRE"

EXPLORING AND SETTLING THE AMERICAN WEST

1803–1869

Books & Maps from the Collection of

J. C. McELVEEN, Jr.

THE GROLIER CLUB

NEW YORK

2018

68

CHASE & BACHELDER'S AMERICAN MUSEUM OF ART

Woodblock poster. Nottingham, England: Stafford & Co., [ca. 1875]. 36½ x 27 in.

This image is one of many that were reproduced or adapted from John Gast's painting *American Progress* (1872). It depicts a female figure towering over settlers and pioneers, and wagons and railroads, as she leads the way westward. It has been interpreted as a representation of Manifest Destiny, the belief that America possessed a right and obligation to expand its boundaries to the Pacific. Here the image was put to a more prosaic use, as the illustration on a poster for an American Museum of Art in England.

CHASE & BACHELDER'S
AMERICAN
MUSEUM OF ART

FOREWORD

THE AMERICAN WEST remained a mysterious region during the early exploration and settlement of North America. Its vast distances, endless rolling grasslands, majestic mountains, imposing tablelands, and countless roiling rivers stirred the imagination of the first explorers and settlers, but slowed their advance.

The exhibition *"Westward the Course of Empire": Exploring and Settling the American West 1803–1869* illustrates this story with contemporary maps and journals from the personal collection of J. C. McElveen, who also curated the event. Following his retirement from a noted Washington, DC law firm, Mr. McElveen augmented his knowledge of western cartography as a volunteer in the Geography and Map Division of the Library of Congress describing its vast collection of early maps of the American West.

Maps are compelling documents for conceptualizing time and space. "Nothing can evoke a moment like a map," Welsh historian and travel writer Jan Morris has written.[1] Geographer Anne Godlewska observed that the map is "a synthesis of information which is a great deal more than just a collection of facts about places."[2]

Prof. Godlewska lists several sources contributing to the power of maps that are relevant to our understanding of early Western exploration and settlement cartography. First, maps illustrate not only what is known or perceived about a place or region but also that which is unknown. Further, since maps convey information pictorially through words, symbols and colors, they are interpreted situationally "as we perceive the world around us" rather than read linearly as a book. This leads to more direct and easier communication with maps than with textual documents. Another characteristic of their power is that map information is greatly generalized in hierarchical form. Coastlines, rivers, paths and roads are straightened; pictorial sketches or contours depict the essential features of mountains and hills. Fourth, maps hold complex and multiple layers of information through words, symbols and colors that illustrate intricate geographical, historical and cultural themes. Next, the precision of the lines and grids on maps suggest a level of scientific accuracy and objectivity that may not always be supported by the subjective nature of nineteenth century cartography. Finally, maps often reflect the biases and belief systems of their producers or patrons, or the particular set of the political, social and economic systems of their era.[3]

---

1. Jan Morris, "On Maps," 5.4 *Asian Art* (Fall, 1992): 3.
2. Anne Godlewska, "Commentary: The Fascination of Jesuit Cartography." In *Jesuit Encounters in the New World: Jesuit Chroniclers, Geographers, Educators and Missionaries in the Americas, 1549–1767,* edited by Joseph A. Gagliano and Charles E. Ronan. Rome: Institutum Historicum S.I., 1997: 99–104.
3. J. Brian Harley, "Deconstruction of the Map," *Cartographia* 26, 2 (1989): 1–20.

1820: Under the Missouri Compromise of 1820, MAINE came into the Union as a free state and MISSOURI came in as a slave state in 1821.

1834: Congress passed *An Act to regulate trade and Intercourse with the Indian tribes, and to preserve peace on the frontiers.* The legislation designated a portion of government-owned land in the West as "Indian Country," and in the statute defined "Indian Country" as "all that part of the United States west of the Mississippi, and not within the states of Missouri and Louisiana, or the territory of Arkansas." By 1836, this area was commonly known as "Indian Territory."

1834–36: THE MICHIGAN TERRITORY was modified yet a third time, to encompass all of what is now MICHIGAN, WISCONSIN and MINNESOTA.

1835: TEXAS declared its independence from Mexico and became a state in 1845.

1836: ARKANSAS became a state.

1836-37: The MICHIGAN TERRITORY was reduced to the current borders of MICHIGAN, and it became a state in 1837.

1836: The WISCONSIN TERRITORY was established and existed until 1838. The boundaries were the old MICHIGAN TERRITORY, except for the current limits of the state of MICHIGAN.

1838: The WISCONSIN TERRITORY was reduced to what are now the current boundaries of WISCONSIN, and THE IOWA TERRITORY was established, and existed, until 1846.

1846: Great Britain and the United States agreed, in the Webster-Ashburton Treaty, to extend the boundary between the United States and Canada along the 49th parallel, to the Pacific Ocean.

1848: OREGON TERRITORY was organized, and was reduced in 1853 by the formation of WASHINGTON TERRITORY. In 1859, OREGON became a state.

1849–58: The northern part of what had been the WISCONSIN TERRITORY existed as the MINNESOTA TERRITORY. IOWA became a state in 1846. WISCONSIN became a state in 1848. MINNESOTA became a state in 1858.

1863: IDAHO TERRITORY was organized from areas taken from WASHINGTON, DAKOTA and NEBRASKA. WASHINGTON became a state in 1889, IDAHO in 1890.

1850: NEW MEXICO TERRITORY was organized. It was taken, in part, from the region transferred to the US from Mexico pursuant to the Treaty of Guadalupe-Hidalgo of 1848, which ended the Mexican War, and in part from land ceded by TEXAS in 1850, under the Compromise of 1850.

1850: UTAH TERRITORY was organized. It included parts of the area acquired from Mexico in the Treaty of Guadalupe-Hidalgo. It was reduced in 1861 by the formation of COLORADO TERRITORY and NEVADA TERRITORY. It was further reduced in 1864 and 1866 by the extension eastward of NEVADA, which would become a state in 1864.

1850: CALIFORNIA became a state. It was a part of the area acquired from Mexico under the Treaty of Guadalupe-Hidalgo.

1854: NEW MEXICO TERRITORY was enlarged by the GADSDEN PURCHASE and then reduced by the formation of the COLORADO TERRITORY in 1861 and the ARIZONA TERRITORY in 1863. NEW MEXICO and ARIZONA became states in 1912.

1854: The remainder of the old LOUISIANA/MISSOURI TERRITORY was split into the KANSAS TERRITORY and the NEBRASKA TERRITORY. KANSAS became a state in 1861. NEBRASKA became a state in 1867 (over a presidential veto).

1858: A concerted effort was made to organize the state of JEFFERSON, to include what is now COLORADO, with small areas in what are now NEBRASKA, WYOMING and UTAH. That failed. COLORADO became a territory in 1861, being made up of parts of the territories of UTAH, NEW MEXICO, KANSAS and NEBRASKA. COLORADO became a state in 1876. UTAH became a state in 1896.

1861: The territory of DAKOTA was organized from parts of MINNESOTA and the NEBRASKA TERRITORY. In 1889, the territory of DAKOTA was divided into NORTH DAKOTA and SOUTH DAKOTA. Later in 1889, NORTH DAKOTA and SOUTH DAKOTA became states.

1864: The territory of MONTANA was organized from a portion of IDAHO TERRITORY and became a state in 1889.

1868: The Territory of WYOMING was organized, becoming a state in 1890.

1890: The OKLAHOMA TERRITORY was organized from the western part of the NATIVE AMERICAN TERRITORY. Additional Native American lands were taken away, including the Cherokee Outlet, and OKLAHOMA became a state in 1907.

My maps and the questions they generated led me to seek out (and, of course, collect) the reports and accounts of these journeys, and to read about the hazards, the triumphs, and the thrills of the westward movement.

"*Westward the Course of Empire*," the title of this catalogue and related exhibition, is borrowed from the first part of the title of a mural displayed in the US Capitol, *Westward the Course of Empire Takes its Way*, by German immigrant painter Emanuel Leutze (1816–68). Completed in 1862, the mural depicts wagon trains of emigrants to the West at an idealized Continental Divide, looking toward a sun-dappled Pacific coast. This mural is one of many visual representations of Manifest Destiny, the theme that runs through this catalogue. The name of the mural is itself a line from a poem by Irish philosopher George Berkeley (1685–1753), "Verses on the Prospect of Planting Arts and Learning in America" (1726).[4]

I hope this catalogue will allow you to come along on this journey west, as you look at the images from early Spanish explorations to Lewis and Clark, to the US Army, to the scientists who helped chart the path for a transcontinental railroad. It has been a great ride for me.

J. C. McElveen

4. Architect of the Capitol. *Compilation of Works of Art and Other Objects in the United States Capitol, 86th Cong., 2nd Sess., House Document No. 162* (Washington, DC: Government Printing Office, 1965). For a more complete discussion of this art, see americanart.si.edu/t2go/1lw/1931.6.1.html (accessed August 13, 2017).

ACKNOWLEDGMENTS

MANY PEOPLE have been extremely helpful to me in bringing this catalogue and exhibition to fruition, and I want to express my everlasting gratitude to them. Ralph Ehrenberg, recently retired chief of the Geography and Map Division of the Library of Congress, and an expert on Lewis and Clark, first stimulated my interest in the mapping of western exploration and showed me many wonders. Anthony Mullan, Diane Schug-O'Neill and Mike Klein, also of the Geography and Map Division, pointed me to fabulous examples of western exploration and mapping. Dealers Barry Lawrence Ruderman, Eliane and Jon Dotson, and Harry Newman have offered me gorgeous examples of important objects, at affordable prices.

This catalogue would never have materialized if it had not been for Fern Cohen, the chair of the Grolier Club Member Exhibitions Committee, who encouraged me to submit a proposal. I also received encouragement and sage advice from Natalie and John Blaney, Tom Touchton and PJ Mode. And I also thank Grolier Club Director Eric Holzenberg and Exhibitions Manager Jennifer Sheehan for their continuing support throughout this endeavor.

I had a great deal of help with my images. Early on, my close friend Larry Rood, photographer par excellence, provided me with a number of very high quality images. Swann Auction Galleries, Barry Lawrence Ruderman Rare Maps, and the Old Print Gallery sent me outstanding high-resolution images. Old World Auctions personnel were kind enough to scan a number of images for me. Franz Jantzen (Archivalman) did some very detailed photos, which have greatly enhanced parts of the catalogue.

As I reviewed catalogues of earlier member exhibits, two names were mentioned in Acknowledgment sections again and again. Those names were George Ong as editor and Jerry Kelly as catalogue designer. Based on the fact that these catalogues were beautifully put together and the text and notes read like a dream, I contacted George and Jerry, and they kindly agreed to help me with this opus. They have been wonderful. What is right about this catalogue is because of them.

Finally, I owe a great debt to my wife, Mary. She put up with my research; she put up with my writing; she read my drafts; she made helpful suggestions. We are still married.

J. C. McELVEEN
August 6, 2017

TYPESET IN
MILLER, BELL & FRY'S ORNAMENTED TYPES.
DESIGN & TYPOGRAPHY BY
JERRY KELLY.

However, there are also features on these maps that are quite accurate or familiar. California is named on maps as early as 1587. Prior to the 1620s, it is shown as a peninsula (as opposed to an island, discussed below). There is some form of a river from the north running into what would later be named the Gulf of California, as the Colorado River would ultimately be shown to do (often, that river is called the Axa River or the Tizon River and is frequently quite short). A river from the east flows into the Gulf of California, which tracks the Gila River pretty well, though that river is often called the River of the Martyrs. The words "Sierra Nevada" (snowy mountains) are used, though they are not always associated with mountains. And "Hispania Nova," or New Spain, is identified (figs. 1 and 2).

CALIFORNIA AS AN ISLAND

Beginning in the early 1620s, perhaps the oddest North American cartographical misrepresentation began to appear on many maps of the West—California as an island. Although very early maps of the Pacific coast of North America showed California, correctly, as being attached to the North American continent, an English mapmaker, Henry Briggs, showed it as an island on a 1625 map, and many mapmakers over the next hundred years followed suit. Briggs may have borrowed the idea from a Spanish map he had seen in the early 1620s, figuring that the Spanish, who had explored much of that part of the world, must know what they were doing. No one is certain why anyone thought California was an island. It is possible that some Spaniards sailed up the Gulf of California, never got as far as the Colorado River and assumed California was an island (figs. 3 and 4). During this period, of course, almost no one knew the exact topography of most of the major land and water features of western North America, and some mapmakers just put features on maps where they thought they ought to be. For example, in a number of maps, though the Mississippi River is shown as emptying out into the Gulf of Mexico, it is shown as doing so from Texas, far west of where its mouth is actually located. Finally, in the late 1600s, Father Eusebio Kino, a Jesuit missionary, traveled from Santa Fe to California, proving that California was not an island. His map, originally published in the *Lettres edifiantes et curieuses, ecrites des missions etrangeres* [Jesuit Letters] (1705) and reprinted many times over the next decades, tried to convey that point visually (fig. 5). However, it was not until the king of Spain decreed in 1746 that California was not an island that the practice of showing it as one was eliminated.

THE 16TH- AND 17TH-CENTURY NORTHWEST

From the very beginnings of exploration of the North American continent there had been a hope, and even an expectation, that there would be a water route across the continent. Initially, it was postulated that the passage would cut across the northern part of the continent, and in many early maps and treatises, it was referred to as the "northwest passage." In one tale, periodically trotted out between 1708 and 1752, a Spanish admiral, Bartholomew de Fonte, was said to have sailed up the west coast of North America in 1650, into a river at 53 degrees north latitude (in present-day British Columbia). As he was sailing east, he encountered a ship heading west from Boston.

As time passed and no passage across the northern part of the continent could be found, it was speculated that perhaps a river flowed across the West and into the Pacific that could easily be accessed, after a short portage, from the source of one of the major eastern rivers. This purported western-flowing river was labeled "River of the West" or the "Buenaventura River," among other names. Though no easy water passage across North America was ever discovered, the legend persisted.

A very popular book and accompanying map by Louis-Armand de Lom d'Arce, Baron de Lahontan (1666–1716) helped keep that myth alive. Baron de Lahontan served in the French army in Canada in the late seventeenth century and was involved in some explorations in present-day Wisconsin. His book, *New Voyages to North-America* (London, 1703), chronicled his adventures in North America. The first part of the work was in the form of rather lengthy letters he purportedly wrote to some colleagues, and one has always been of particular interest: Letter XVI (Missilimakinac, May 28, 1689). There he described a trip he took, in 1688, down the Mississippi River and then northwest up another large river, for several hundred miles. He called this river the Longue River, or the Morte River. He told of meeting up along this river with Native Americans from a tribe he called the Gnacsitares, who described another, very aggressive tribe, located further west, called the Mozeemlek. Four Mozeemlek captives provided him with "a description of their country," with their villages standing "upon a [westward-flowing] river that springs out of a ridge of mountains from which the long river also derives its source."[5] The captives proceeded to tell Lahontan that the river on which they lived emptied "it self into a Salt Lake of three hundred leagues in circumference." The letter went on to describe the mountains of which the Mozeemleks spoke as being "six leagues broad and so high that one must cast an Infinity of Windings and Turnings before he can cross 'em."[6] The map that accompanied these descriptions even showed the portage from the source of the eastward-flowing "Longue River" to the westward-flowing river (fig. 6).

There is no documentation for Baron de Lahontan's trip, only his word that it occurred, and many believe that his was just another tall tale. However, some scholars have opined that he may well have had contact with Native Americans who told him about the height and ruggedness of the Rocky Mountains and described the Great Salt Lake of Utah. In any event, his book and map served to perpetuate the belief that there was a river route across much of the North American continent.

---

5. Louis-Armand de Lom d'Arce, Baron Lahontan, *New Voyages to North America*, vol. 1, 2nd ed. (London: John Brindley, 1735), 124–5.
6. Ibid.